NOT JUST FURRY DICE...

NOT JUST FURRY DICE...

LIFE IN THE FAST LANE
OF CAR ACCESSORIES

CHRIS MITCHELL

Matador
9 Priory Business Park,
Wistow Road, Kibworth Beauchamp,
Leicestershire. LE8 0RX
Tel: 0116 279 2299
Email: books@troubador.co.uk
Web: www.troubador.co.uk/matador
Twitter: @matadorbooks

In co-operation with The Black Cat Partnership Ltd

ISBN 978 1800465 329

British Library Cataloguing in Publication Data.
A catalogue record for this book is available from the British Library.

Printed and bound in the UK by TJ Books Limited, Padstow, Cornwall
Typeset in 11pt Adobe Garamond Pro by Troubador Publishing Ltd, Leicester, UK

Matador is an imprint of Troubador Publishing Ltd

To Rosie Mitchell, 1969-1994

"Wit and fortitude filled her short life"

FOREWORD BY PADDY HOPKIRK MBE

 I have known Chris for longer than I care to remember. From the past car accessory shop I had in Peterborough and my manufacturing years which followed, he used to contact me with new and often unique product ideas – some very good and some a bit of a gamble …

As our resources and ideas for testing things out were limited, it was a guessing game. We used to launch new products and wait to see if they were winners or not. This was all great fun at the time but a bit amateurish compared with today's market research-driven product development.

At the car accessory shows the customers always used to ask, "What have you got that's new?" All very different from today, as it was long before the coming of the Internet and social media.

Chris was always a very friendly, charming man, with time to listen – and he was also a good, trustworthy businessman.

Paddy Hopkirk

AUTHOR'S NOTE

Apologies in advance if certain aspects of this book seem somewhat sexist and a little un-PC, but bear in mind that the story ends nearly three decades ago at the time of writing.

The contents are neither intended to be any sort of personal autobiography, nor a definitive history of the rise and fall of that part of an industry that came to be known as the 'lunatic fringe' of the motor trade. It's more of a light-hearted romp through 30 interesting and often challenging years.

Chris Mitchell
December 2020

ONE

IGNITION

T WAS 1992 AND AT AN AIRPORT IN TEXAS, ON 22 AUGUST, William M Jeter III, president of Petrolon Inc., Houston, was refusing to board his executive jet – destination UK – until his lawyers told him that the Mitchell deal was ready for signing.

In Leicester, England, it was around midnight on the same day in the conference rooms of a hotel beside the M1 motorway. Five lawyers, four accountants, two bankers, my two directors and four secretaries had spent four continuous days and nights wrangling over endless pages of smallprint. Finally everyone agreed: "OK, that's it. Tell him yes. Get over here!"

I could only then start to relax and reflect on what a lot had happened in the 32 years since I had given notice to end three tedious years as a lowly management trainee with Sketchley Ltd, the national dry-cleaning chain based in Hinckley, Leicestershire. Having had four tough years at a boarding school in Surrey, it was a major culture change when I started working a trouser press on £9 a week, but at least it gave me an income.

Perhaps, unusually in my late teens, I had displayed little interest in motorcars. Certainly I was driving to work from Leicester to

Hinckley in a 1935 Austin 7 Ruby, which I had bought for the significant sum of £35. But this had been a sensible economy, except when breakdowns forced me back onto the sluggish train service from Leicester.

I confess that my enthusiasm for the car was not unconnected with my much greater enthusiasm for the opposite sex and the consequent opportunities for seclusion that car ownership brought with it. Living at home with my mother and younger brother, supported by my grandfather following the death of my father in the Second World War, could be rather claustrophobic in social terms, so the car became a valuable asset. The only trouble was that the 5lbs oil pressure dropped to zero after the first five miles over the 15-mile commute and splash lubrication miraculously got me to Hinckley each time.

Events took an interesting turn when I was offered a regular lift by a much more senior Sketchley executive, who lived nearby. This was a real eye-opener, as he had a Triumph TR2 and for the first time in my life I was driven by him – extremely fast – and felt the thrill of cornering 'on the door handles'. This was a big change from our sedate family Austin A40 Somerset, which rarely exceeded 50mph.

My new friend also raced at the weekends at Silverstone, in an HRG Lea Francis single seater. This car, which had a pre-selector gearbox, had no self starter, so required a push from four strong men and also had to be warmed up with the rear wheels jacked up off the ground. It was always a drama in the paddock with the four open-stub exhaust pipes belching flame. Added to that was the deafening noise and also the highly evocative smell of Castrol R vegetable-based racing oil, which was intoxicating. Even today Castrol R is still used in some vintage cars and I'm sure it would go down a storm as an aftershave aroma even now amongst a certain generation.

My addiction was further fuelled when, a year or so later, my newfound friend decided that the recently launched Morris Mini would make a good track car. It was the very early days of what became a hugely popular and exciting class, but I vividly recall his acquiring and then entering his first race in a Mini, simply minus hubcaps and carpets and with a different needle in the carburettor. He found it huge fun and my craving for motorsport and everything connected was ignited.

The launch of the Mini in 1958 had been a major event, but an even greater one for me was an unexpected bequest from a relative, which, when added to my savings, suddenly enabled me to purchase a brand new, Surf Blue Mini for £498. I bought the car from Frank Taylor Ltd, a garage in Hinckley and it made my trip to work both reliable and far more fun. I sold the old Austin Ruby to a friend for the same price I had paid for it – just as well, as the half-shafts snapped a week later.

The boys racing the Minis soon found that the little cream-coloured, ten-inch pressed steel wheels were starting to fly off across the track. The high cornering forces were more than they could stand, with the wheel nuts and studs pulling right through the metal. This sparked demand for thicker, lighter, alloy wheels, which was soon satisfied by Dunlop, Cosmic and others, although they weren't a necessity for the weekly shop. A brand new industry was being born.

The early Minis were notorious for dubious build quality and on one occasion the gearlever came right out of its slot in the floor as I was changing gear. I was so shocked that to this day I can't remember what happened next …

Although Volvo was the first company to actually fit lap and diagonal safety belts in 1959, it wasn't until the early 60s that the first safety belts appeared on the market and I was one of the first to buy a set of Britax-manufactured seatbelts for the front seats. In those days, busy junctions didn't always have traffic lights, only a policeman on point duty at rush hour. Heading back home one evening, I was halted by the raised hand of the officer on duty in the middle of a main crossroads. As I waited to turn right, he suddenly knocked on the window, which I nervously slid open. "That cross belt you are wearing, sir; is it to stop you hitting the steering wheel in a collision?" I could only reply yes, whereupon he added: "It's a pity more people don't have them. Off you go then". He then stopped the traffic and sent me on my way.

I spent more and more time at weekends being taken to various circuits and soon I was introduced to another local driver, Robin Sturgess. He was the son of Frank Sturgess, who ran the highly successful Jaguar and Land Rover distributorship for Leicestershire, W.E. Sturgess and Sons Ltd, which latterly also held the Royal Warrant.

Driving a Jaguar was the symbol of success in those post-war days, when buying a German or Japanese car was seen as somewhat unpatriotic. Robin sported a fashionable moustache, rode to hounds and was the archetypal dashing young man about Leicestershire. He was an enthusiastic amateur racing driver, encouraged by Jaguar Cars and supported by the family business. When I first came to know him he was racing the iconic C-Type Jaguar and becoming very well known on the circuits and was even paid starting money for one event.

An aside to the main firm and as a personal investment, he had opened Leicestershire's first speed shop, Robin Sturgess Accessories, just across the road from the car business, at 169 Walnut Street, Leicester. It carried an eclectic stock of motor racing-themed wastepaper baskets, tablemats, cufflinks and ties. This was all mixed in with products from the Les Leston motoring catalogue, including chequered flag umbrellas, racing seats, wood-rimmed steering wheels, driving shoes and crash helmets. Les Leston was the 1954 Formula 3 champion. He had driven in the Le Mans 24-hour race and was the first big 'go-faster' goods supplier.

However, the hapless local, very elderly, lady recruited to run the shop had not the slightest idea about most of the products in store. Robin realised he needed a proper enthusiast to serve keen young motorists after the memorable time a customer asked her whether they stocked any pistons for Minis. She understood the part of the description involving cylindrical shiny things, but then appeared with a paper bag containing four chrome-plated exhaust trims.

Sketchley had just offered me my first promotion to assistant district manager over 30 shops in Leicestershire, on condition, however, that I was married. This was on the basis that it would otherwise be improper to be in charge of 30 manageresses unless made respectable and focussed by marriage.

Enough was enough and to my surprise Robin then offered me the job of running the shop, until he found out that by then I was earning £12 a week. "Ridiculous – quite unaffordable, old lad. How about 2% of sales instead?" There hardly were any sales, but being bored and unmarried, I took it – very appropriate, as Cliff Richard had just reached No.1 in the hit parade with *Batchelor Boy*.

With the shop now established, my new boss's next job was to dump the old C-Type Jaguar. Deliveries to the family firm over the road of the new E-Type were only weeks away and it was rumoured to be an absolute stunner, offering massive improvements. So, a quarter-page advert in *Motor Sport* for car and trailer, price £1,000, achieved a quick and welcome sale of the old C-Type.

More petrol-headed readers will know that the C-Type Jaguar was a rare beast and in the subsequent years of massive inflation of the value of vintage racing cars, it rapidly became one of the world's most sought-after classics. Moving on 56 years to 2016, that very same car was auctioned by Bonhams in Monte Carlo. They produced a 14-page feature in the sale catalogue and with Robin present as guest of honour, the famous ex-Sturgess C-Type sold for nearly six million Euros, plus tax and commission.

So my boss was ready to be one of the first to race the new E-Type and I was really eager to run his little shop, with five O-Levels, no experience of business whatsoever – and no guaranteed income.

My first task was to sell a job lot of a gross of unwisely bought 'Turbo Visors', purchased before I had started. This product had shot to prominence in the press after Britain's top driver, Graham Hill, was photographed testing one, driving a grand prix car on track, on a very wet day at Silverstone. This strange device had a transparent, circular, vaned visor disc, mounted in the centre of an alloy helmet bracket, with a ball bearing in front of the driver or rider's nose. This would spin water off very effectively at speeds over 90mph. The trouble was that below that speed the user had virtually no vision, so on the road only the very bravest of racers or motorcyclists could reach speeds enabling them to see anything at all and it could be dangerous to slow down. This was a tough sell and we only ever sold three! *First lesson: get the buying right.*

Among our product range was a combined seat-stick/umbrella with a chequered flag design. The only problem was that the alloy hinges supporting the foldout handles, which also formed the seat of the shooting stick, were very fragile and apt to snap off as soon as anyone substantial sat on them – with the result that the customer could become nearly impaled. Problem solved by refund rather than surgery. *Second lesson: ensure customer satisfaction.*

The shop's location in the midst of a network of residential side streets, surrounded by rows of terraced houses, meant that locals often tried us on the off chance for torch batteries, which we didn't sell. One day, a middle-aged lady came in and I thought "torch batteries", only to be astounded when she requested flameproof underwear, overalls and a crash helmet, plus the latest thin-soled racing boots. It turned out she was Mrs. Bluebell-Gibbs, a famous amateur racing driver of the day. *Third lesson: don't judge by first appearances.*

In those days, few speed shops sold anything in the way of polish, shampoos, leak sealants, or indeed any bottled or canned products for cars. One day, a slick-looking salesman called in selling a canned engine oil additive called STP. I initially rejected it, as I couldn't see much need; the only stuff that went in the family Austin was a penny shot of Redex, squirted into the petrol tank by the petrol pump attendant. Anyway, we didn't sell stuff in cans or bottles, but I then relented and on his next visit I bought a case of 24.

The stuff sold very quickly. It turned out that STP had a hugely visible oval logo all over some of the famous American dragsters, which were just hitting the motoring headlines for their shattering acceleration, so it was beginning to gain considerable attention in the UK. Ten years later we were still selling huge quantities of STP, until it became my biggest competitor, but that's for later …

Most accessory shops in the 1960s were finding their feet and although the very small terraced house we were in had a shop window fitted and the ground floor knocked through and carpeted, it was all very decrepit behind the scenes. At the back, the plumbing had in fact collapsed beneath the kitchen flooring, making it unusable. To get at the sink to fill the kettle you needed to straddle a large hole in the middle of the floor.

The non-existent plumbing also meant that calls of nature could not be properly answered, except by running across the busy road to the Jaguar service dept. This was fine, except in continuous rush-hour traffic when considerable bladder control was required.

A growing and extremely varied stock mix included Tudor windscreen washer kits – luxuries not deemed essential and certainly not compulsory. Indeed, a factory ordered heater for an MGB in the '60s cost an extra £15. Radiator muffs were a good line, made mostly in rubber, each shaped for different radiator grilles. But as model changes became more frequent and thermostats more efficient, they were doomed.

A steady line of business came from stretch over, Bri-Nylon seat covers by Karobes and Kumficar, often paired with garish, fluffy 'ocelot' leopard pattern, elasticated steering wheel gloves. Thankfully, these were soon superceded by more sophisticated black or tan leather, lace-on steering wheel covers by Cosmic, which appealed much more to sportier motorists.

Also in demand were tan, string-backed driving gloves and thin, black and red, Graham Hill leather gloves with knuckle holes. By 1964, headrests were growing in popularity, even though they were just a wire-upholstered frame pushed over the back of the seat with a nicely padded front – hopeless in an accident, but comfy for the show-off.

By no means, even in 1968, did all cars have heaters and demisters, but you could obtain a foot-long Bakelite strip with a heating element and twin-suction cups either end. Whilst this could move a bit of misty condensation given half an hour, it needed two hours and a flat battery to clear a frosted up windscreen. Matching fog and spotlights by Lucas and Raydyot were a popular add-on, as were the highly flashy, black and white-chequered, padded lamp covers.

When Alex Issigonis designed the Mini for BMC in the 1950s, as a small family car, little did he know what he had started. While history tells us that BMC made only about £6 on each car, the fortunes made by those selling bits for Minis has been vast. It began very simply. The whole central speedometer cluster and the small row of switches beneath were very far forward and the driver sat quite far back, making it a real stretch to reach the wiper and light switches. A three-inch section of plastic tubing to push over each switch stalk solved the problem, nicely packaged for two and sixpence, and the Mini bits business began to flourish.

All except the shortest drivers needed a bit more legroom and started buying seat extension brackets to add another rearwards three inches. This left the steering wheel a bit of a reach away, so a nifty bracket dropped it more neatly towards the driver. Lo and behold, the gear lever now needed a short, screw-on extension and at the same time let's fit a nice wooden gear knob ...

Soon, proper door handles to replace the plastic-covered wire pulls in the doors appeared and famous Monte Carlo Rally winning driver Paddy Hopkirk was in on the act with a range of bits, including most of these, but uniquely a larger ribbed aluminium pedal extension for the Mini's rather puny, one-inch square accelerator pad.

He then introduced radiator grille-release buttons, leather bonnet straps and sump guards. Impressive full-width moulded dashboards, by Mada, ready to fill with extra instruments, were highly sought after, as well as jazzier, shiny radiator grilles; then came hugely popular wheel spacers, easily fitted between brake drum and hub to push the wheels out wider for a lairier look.

With wheels now projecting too far out and falling foul of the law, the next necessity was wheel arch extensions and of course the Mini's higher cornering speeds required better positioning for the driver, so not only did black-padded seat covers with built-up sides appear, but beautifully padded, grippy, fiberglass-moulded racing seats. Made by Corbeau, Restall and Terry Hunter, among others, these were much envied as an addition to the cockpit.

Before the launch of the Mini Cooper, drivers had to wrestle with a long, whippy gearstick sprouting from the footboard on the floor and soon a remote control gear change, concealed by a handsome plastic moulding, was made by SPQR Engineering. This sold like mad, becoming our most expensive product, at £25.

The Italians were ahead of the game, with air horns working off a compressor and made by Maserati and Fiamm. Wealthier drivers didn't just have to have the deafening double trumpet single blast. Now four, five and six trumpet versions appeared, offering such tunes as *The Wedding March, Colonel Bogey, La Cucaracha and Never on a Sunday*. However, alternating two-tone horns, both then and now, remain illegal and confined to the emergency services. Strangely, more than two are still permissible.

As their popularity snowballed, complaints about these noisy distractions grew and eventually ATV in the West Midlands asked me over to their Birmingham studios. Here they had set up a full selection of horns to accentuate the nuisance value of our 'shocking' products and a rather aggressive interview was conducted amongst a cacophony of sound. I never saw the actual transmission, as it aired at 6pm and I didn't get home until 7pm – no recorders then. Anyway, it worked wonders for sales.

Other popular noisemakers for cars were the piercing, 'girl-baiting' Wolf-Whistle, which used the suction from the inlet manifold, with the driver pulling a wire, and the Bullhorn, a realistic, deep bellow, generated by an electrical diaphragm in a red housing. Pedestrians always looked round for the charging beast.

I always held a psychological theory to excuse the fitting of many products: that of 'avoiding the previous owner's contact points'. Buying an often very much-used car inevitably left lingering memories of the previous owner sitting there, handling all the knobs and switches, whilst using it for years. If you could therefore replace the gear knob, steering wheel, seat covers and floor mats, the car immediately shed its tactile association with the driver before you. Change the contact points and the car really is yours – and that was exactly what was happening.

TWO

INTO GEAR

THERE IS REALLY ONLY ONE SURE WAY TO IMPROVE engine breathing and that is with a proper free-flow exhaust manifold. But in the early boy-racer days this was way beyond the reach of most. Instead, a Peco or Speedwell big-bore silencer gave instant street cred, with huge, oversized tailpipes and a sporty, 'rorty' exhaust note. A much cheaper alternative, which could be fitted in ten minutes, was the Peco exhaust booster, or the Alexpress exhaust extractor. You simply cut four inches off the tailpipe and clamped it on. This looked and sounded really good, but had no effect at all, although it came in a very handsome illustrated box and was an absolute 'must' for younger show-offs.

The biggest money-spinner of all was the replacement steering wheel. Even in 1960 the Moto-Lita wood rim steering wheel was available, but it came with an expensive price tag. The mass market really took off around 1962, when Les Leston introduced the separate wood rim, in a variety of diameters, with interchangeable aluminium bosses to fit onto all different types of steering column, spanning every make and model of car.

Retailers simply needed a good stock of boss kits and a smaller selection of wheel rims. It was then easy to line up the rims and bosses, tighten up six small bolts, a dab of Locktite, two minutes with a screwdriver and job done. But it still needed fitting to the car. Soon, almost every small car and sports car driver aspired to a sportier, smaller steering wheel. Then came the black leather version – even sexier and grippier. Before long, spiralling demand spawned versions from Mountney, Cosmic, Formula and Astrali, but the very first on the market, Moto-Lita, almost the sole survivor, is still going strong after 60 years.

Air fresheners were always popular, although not of course with the real rally boys. The 'Traffic Light' version from Polco was a favourite, but nothing beat so-called 'Smelly Trees', a pine tree-shaped and pine smelling cardboard cut-out – still on sale in 2021 – another rare survivor. Window tint aerosol sprays did really well until the police clamped down on people predictably spraying ALL the windows to add a sinister shaded look, even before the days of drug dealers. Briefly, when the 70mph limit was introduced by transport Minister Ernest Marples in December 1965, there was a flurry of enthusiasm for 'Marples Must Go' rear window stickers. We never turned down a sale. Before long, Hella came up with an easily wired-in kit to delay windscreen wiper sweeps – very popular – as was fitting a switch to make all the indicator lights flash at the same time in an emergency, but yet another novelty then!

THE BULLET HOLE SAGA

In early 1964, I read that an American company was producing stick-on 'bullet holes' for the film industry, but on further inquiry drew a blank, as they refused to do export, as did most American firms in those days.

Having a hunch that a line of 'bullet holes' across the rear window of a car would be a fun product in those less violent times, we got a local artist to produce a copy of the American design and showed it to a local printer, Wills and Co. in Churchgate, Leicester. They suggested a strip of three could be printed as waterslide transfers and quoted a penny a set for a minimum quantity of 1,000 sets. I thought two shillings would be a good retail price, leaving plenty of margin if we needed motor trade distribution, so we went for it. The handful of trade outlets we were supplying with steering wheels all bought some, applied them to their own cars – and immediately reordered. I did a sales blitz on some local filling stations with bundles of our Bulletholes displayed on a backing card and we were away with our very first 'in-house' product. How times have changed – gun crime levels now make it far from a joke.

About this time, being mainly stuck in the shop, I needed two things: some firm's transport and a secretary/shop assistant. The first came in the shape of a very secondhand Minivan, which we had sign written and added a black and white chequered roof. The second requirement came in the shapely form of Nollie Noel-Key, a very lively young blonde I had met at a party one Saturday night. Her main qualifications were typing, a friendly manner and the ability to start that Monday morning. Bulletholes were her first job, as each strip of three had to be hand stamped on the back with the instructions, so Nollie's tasks were rubber-stamping thousands of Bulletholes, doing my typing, (men couldn't type in those days) and serving in the shop.

The first Bullethole printing was quickly repeated, but then came the big breakthrough. Someone tipped off the News of the World, who somehow got wind of the police reacting to a false alarm about a car, seemingly having been in a shootout. The next Sunday they did a half-page splash, having interviewed a vicar with Bulletholes across the back windows of his Morris Minor Traveller. They roundly condemned us in bold headlines for wasting police time – brilliant – and away we went with another reprint, this time for 10,000 strips.

A freelance journalist then came to Leicester and staged photographs of Robin Sturgess holding a gun, firing at my assistant's Mini. The writer asked for permission to translate and syndicate a feature worldwide, which we were certainly not going to refuse and the orders came piling in from all over the world. We even had a fair few envelopes addressed simply to 'The Bullethole Company, Leicester England'. Even the BBC's Biddy Baxter wrote in asking for samples, which were then shown on the *Blue Peter* programme.

It did no harm that the third James Bond film, *Goldfinger*, had just been launched. We encouraged our trade customers to refer to the James Bond 'bullet holes' and even used 007 on one of our posters. Never did we consider that licence fees might be involved.

Another legal issue we only just avoided was being sued by The British Motor Corporation. We had, with a minor change, copied their 'Works Team' rosette logo, which appeared on the wings of the works rally cars in the Monte Carlo Rally and these were selling well. Then a solicitor's letter arrived from BMC's lawyer accusing us of 'passing off' and telling us to destroy all stocks, or we would be in court. Luckily, we only had a dozen left, so no problem.

To do a proper job we felt that our Bulletholes needed to continue across the bodywork, so we brought out a version with curly metal edges and a black centre, still two shillings a strip. Whilst we had posted small quantities all over the world, we were surprised when a seemingly well connected company in Sweden asked for exclusive rights in Scandinavia, subject to an executive visiting them with 1,000 sets and authority to sign a deal.

In December 1965, Robin was booked to go and meet them at a town called Hudiksvaal, north of Upsala, near the Arctic Circle, but he went down suddenly with flu, so I flew to Sweden carrying 1,000 Bulletholes. I then took a lengthy train ride up north, where I agreed to an exclusive deal and a credit account. My first business trip abroad was another salutary lesson, as they never paid us. Even so, by then we were producing a monthly *Bullethole Bulletin* and sales were ever increasing.

Eventually the gravy train stopped when multinational Regent Petroleum, with hundreds of filling stations, printed their own 'bullet holes' and gave them away with five gallons of petrol. To put the lid on it, Esso then started the 'Put a Tiger in Your Tank' campaign and gave away free fluffy tiger tails with five gallons of petrol – a craze that soon eclipsed ours.

(Top) *Author's first car with "rabbit's ears" flashers.*
(Bottom Left) *Volvo were first with seat belts.*
(Bottom Right) *Early mini racers.*

(Top) *"C" Type Jaguar sells well.*
(Middle) *Big brand oil additive*
(Bottom) *Graham Hill with the Turbovisor.*

Les Leston Exclusive Motor Racing Umbrella
Standard "golf" size panelled in international racing flag signals. Lightweight metal frame, shaft and spike. Guaranteed fully waterproof.
E6/1

Folding Seat Umbrella
Lightweight aluminium frame, folding seat, aluminium shaft and spike. Guaranteed fully waterproof.
E6/5

(Top) ...*and fluffy wheel gloves to match.*
(Middle) *Could be painful!*
(Bottom Left) *Hot silencers sold like hot cakes.*

PADDY
HOPKIRK
MOTOR
ACCESSORIES

LES
LESTON

*Motor
Racing
Equipment*

GO WELL · GO SHELL

(Top) *First "company" car.*
(Middle & Bottom) *Goody packed catalogues.*

"RALLY" PADDED SEAT COVER

£6/6/0
Colour Black

(Top) *Oh so grippy.*
(Bottom) *Very safe up to walking pace.*

(Top Left) *Early belt supplier.*
(Top Right) *Instant knock-on wheels.*
(Bottom) *Bull's come-hither bellow, risky in dairy farm.*

BULL HORN
A full-noted highway horn which gives a realistic bull-like bellow. The Jubilee horn is louder than most twin horns and can be sounded loud and soft. The steering post up-and-down control gives a novel rolling tone. In red enamel finish and measuring 8″ x 5″ x 6½″. Comes complete with variable pitch steering post control, mounting kit and full instructions.
Part No. 118

All the kit, ready to fit.

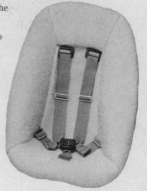
(Top) *Easily fitted – easily ejected.* (Bottom) *Things soon improved.*

(Top) *Instant street cred.* (Bottom) *For motoring tipplers.*

Ambassadors: *Two of the vans which Robin Sturgess Accessories are using on their three-weekly delivery scheme for garages in the Midlands and South Midlands. Robin Sturgess, of 169 Walnut Street, Leicester, are distributors for Cibie, Les Leston, Alexander, Speedwell, Peco and many others.*

GRAHAM HILL DRIVING GLOVES FOR GIRLS

Finest quality Pittards Leather guaranteed washable and colourfast. Specially designed by Graham Hill to combine maximum control with a dash of elegance for sport and everyday motoring. Vent holes in fingers, semi-open back and "Velcro" touch 'n' close fastening. Colours: Black with Red or White trim. Sizes 6½, 7, 7½.

52/6 PAIR

35/-

SUNGLASSES
Finest quality black/white chequered frames combined with optically corrected lenses make these the most fabulous accessory of the year. An absolute must for all motoring enthuisasts.

(Top) *The fleet increases.*
(Bottom Left) *Oh so Mary Quant.*
(Bottom Right) *Ten inch Minilites, the ultimate wheel.*

Maserati Air Horns

T. S. SPRINT.

A really loud horn for penetrating, discordant, high-noted blast. Ideal for motorway and Continental driving. It incorporates a new, extra-powerful compressor which is available only with Maserati horns. A pair of tough red plastic trumpets 6¼" long with a base diameter of 3". The base incorporates a revolutionary new design feature which effectively guards against moisture or water damage to horns. Compressor height 4½", diameter 2¼". The TS Sprint will fit under the bonnet of any car and comes complete with relay, tubing, fixing nuts and bolts, and full instructions. 6, 12, or 24 volts. Also available with chrome plated metal trumpets.

Air Horns

T.S. Plastic	6 volt	Part No. 066
T.S. Plastic	12 volt	Part No. 067
T.S. Plastic	24 volt	Part No. 068
T.S. Chrome	6 volt	Part No. 069
T.S. Chrome	12 volt	Part No. 070
T.S. Chrome	24 volt	Part No. 071

T. N. NORMAL.

This horn is just as powerful as the T.S. Sprint but the note is mellower and less discordant. It gains immediate attention without startling. It incorporates the extra-powerful Maserati compressor. The tough red plastic trumpets are 6½" and 8¼" long respectively. The bases are 3" diameter and incorporate a revolutionary new design feature which effectively guards against moisture or water damage to horns. Compressor height 4½", diameter 2¼". Complete with relay, tubing, fixing nuts and bolts, and full instructions. 6, 12 or 24 volts. Available in plastic or chrome.

Air Horns

T.N. Plastic	6 volt	Part No. 072
T.N. Plastic	12 volt	Part No. 073
T.N. Plastic	24 volt	Part No. 074
T.N. Chrome	6 volt	Part No. 075
T.N. Chrome	12 volt	Part No. 076
T.N. Chrome	24 volt	Part No. 077

T.3 MINOR.

This pleasant musical horn has a flick-over switch which enables you to sound the three notes in quick succession or in unison. The extra-tough plastic trumpets are 6¼", 8¼", and 9¼" long respectively. The bases are 3" diameter and incorporate a revolutionary new design feature which effectively guards against moisture or water damage to horns. Compressor height 6¼", diameter 2¼". T.3 Minor comes complete with relay, tubing, switch, fixing nuts and bolts, and full instructions. 6 or 12 volts. Available in plastic or chrome.

Air Horns

T.3. Minor Plastic	6 volt	Part No. 078
T.3. Minor Plastic	12 volt	Part No. 079
T.3. Minor Chrome	6 volt	Part No. 080
T.3. Minor Chrome	12 volt	Part No. 081

Harry Moss (London) Limited, 424 Kingston Road, London, SW20 8LJ. 01-540 8131

*The longer tunes needed seven trumpets
and a lot of under bonnet space.*

Cross their palms with leather

– the leather of a Mountney steering wheel.

Let their eyes take in the three polished aluminium spokes (slotted or plain) and the one piece thumb spats. The thing they perhaps won't discern immediately is the much tested rim section and proven construction but when you show them the range — 10", 11", 12", 13" & 14" sizes in flat/semi dished or deep dish — show them the makes of British European & Continental cars that Mountney wheels fit — then tell them the price.

You'll be amazed how fast they'll cross your palms with silver.

Mountney steering wheels have black leather trim and polished aluminium as standard. A range of coloured leathers and anodised aluminiums are available on request.

Write or phone and we'll tell you more about our discounts and what's in it for you.

RRP £12·96 incl. VAT
Export enquiries welcome

Mountney Motor Products,
3 Rose Way, Purdeys Industrial Estate,
Rochford, Essex, England.
Telephone: Southend (0702) 547434

Auto Accessory Retailer January 1977

inquiry card ref. 230

THE FABULOUS LES LESTON

The Les Leston Grand Prix Steering Wheel is the most elegant wood rim wheel in the world. It gives greater driving comfort, better instrument vision and is stronger and safer. The highly polished mahogany wood rim is contoured to fit the hand with correctly positioned finger grooves on the underside. The aluminium spokes are polished and the edges safely rounded. There is a full circle of metal concealed beneath the wood and joined to the spokes to give complete security and maximum strength. All wood and metal parts are epoxy resin bonded to withstand any climatic conditions.

Austin Healey Sprite Mk. I and II
BMC Mini and 1100 range
Ford Cortina and Corsair up to 1965
Hillman Imp
Lotus Cortina and Elan
MGA and 1600
MG Midget Mk. I
Morris Minor 1000
Porsche 356 B/C
Riley 1·5
Riley Elf
Rover 2000
Singer Chamois
Triumph Herald and Vitesse
Spitfire, TR4 and 4A
Wolseley 1500
Wolseley Hornet

£7/9/6

(Leather covered £8/4/6)

SAVE MONEY – all LES LESTON GOODS are sent **POST FREE!** (UK ONLY)

2

Just two of many "wheeler dealers".

The Motacoat

Made by Goldex of Leicester
in double thickness wool/cotton mixture
for extreme warmth.

Side and top pockets.

Washable anti-corrosive zip.

Raglan sleeves, knitted windproof cuffs.

Chest sizes in **38″ 40″ 42″**

£4 : 4 : 0

**The Robin Sturgess
Rally Jacket**

Made exclusively for Robin Sturgess
by Bennett Morris of Manchester,
in quilted showerproof nylon.
Touch and close front fastening,
roll collar contains a hood.
Also with stop watch cord,
pencil pockets, etc.
In British Racing Green with Gold
lining, button sleeves and waist.
Small, Medium, Large, Extra Large

£8 : 8 : 0

Robin Sturgess Accessories

169 Walnut Street, Leicester   Telephone: Leicester 58551

Our first flyer – unaware that it might be misinterpreted!

(Top) *Paddy Hopkirk with his new GT Wheels.*
(Bottom) *Roger Clark and Tony Mason in works Escort lit by Cibié Oscars.*

(Bottom) *The B.M.C. rosette – our version.*

Protex Flameproof Grand Prix Driving Boots

This is the latest addition to the Les Leston range of protective clothing. Protex boots have an interior lining of flameproof material and the 'non-slip' chrome leather soles are naturally flame resistant as are the uppers. Made from finest quality materials throughout. Soles and uppers have flush edges to eliminate possibility of getting caught up beneath car pedals. The boots are specially designed for wearing in cars with close pedal arrangements and limited space for feet. There is a fibre pressure plate built into the soles and the extended heel rest prevents wear and eliminates dangerous projections.

Colour Black
All sizes from 6 to 12½

D2/6/add SIZE

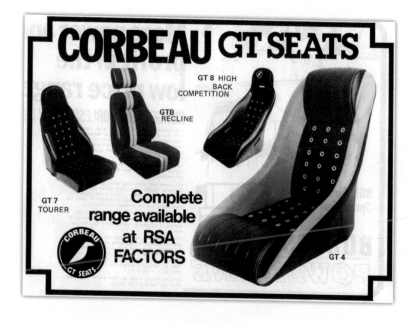

What a combination – racing boots and bucket seats.

Highly illegal today.

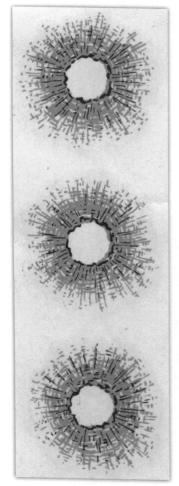

Sales soon shot up.

We soon became exporters.

Robin Sturgess helping with sales.

(Bottom) *Graham Hill opens new Abbey lane premises.*
Left: Robin, Right: Author.

THE NEW GRAHAM HILL RALLYMASTER JACKET!

The Graham Hill 'Rallymaster' Jacket has been specially designed by Graham to meet the needs not only of the Sporting Motorist and Professional Rally Driver but for ALL men who want a lightweight jacket giving the ultimate in freedom combined with maximum winter warmth.

The 'Rallymaster' is fully waterproof being made of 'Dunloprufe Bri-Nylon'. Completely washable and windproof. With 'Courtelle' quilting.

Not only worn by Graham Hill but also by the world's leading Race and Rally Drivers.

SUPERB QUALITY AND STYLING FULLY GUARANTEED

Les Leston Ltd.,
314 High Holborn, London, W.C.1
CHAncery 8655/6/7
Cables: Gofaster, London, W.C.1

(Bottom) *Two more new vans, note Ford Anglia 105E front on roof rack.*

(Bottom) *Staff and directors on opening of*
Freeman's Common premises, in 1975.

Much referred to by the trade, 30 pages to update monthly was becoming a chore.

As the '60s progressed a plethora of products became available: replacement gear lever knobs in wood and alloy, supplementary instruments, especially rev counters, and then suddenly a new development was upon us, auxiliary lighting, but with a twist …

The exciting new quartz iodine bulb provided vastly greater, piercing white light output than the old tungsten bulbs and immediately the big French lighting manufacturers, Cibié, and Marchal were offering the latest thing in long-range spotlights. When the word got round, enthusiastic motorists flocked into the shop to see these fearsome light projectors. My salesman's reply, when asked about beam distance, was to say, "Up to two miles under laboratory conditions", or, "You must never stand in front when they're switched on, as they can burn your eyeballs out". Sale absolutely guaranteed! The Cibié Super Oscars were the ultimate, but would never have reached the UK market without the business acumen of Charles Meisl, who set up Britover Ltd as the importers. He was also a world famous balloonist, but goes down in history for selling the very first Porsche on UK soil in January 1954 via AFN motors in London.

The works rally teams were all now wearing the iconic black Dunlop rally jackets, featuring a long, bold yellow sleeve stripe, as well as the first use of a Velcro front-fastening. Once we had sourced these, everyone wanted one and before long we had our own made in dark green with a smart yellow lining and yellow sleeve stripes. This also justified our first dedicated colour leaflet, which caused a few ribald comments … it never struck us at the time.

INTERNATIONAL RACING CAR SHOW

We now felt like a bit of a gamble and wanted some national exposure. The International Racing Car Show had just moved from London's Horticultural Halls to Olympia, so we signed up for the 1964 show, which promised rewarding results.

For this great experiment we had a portable counter constructed with retractable handles in the four corners, shelved storage space and a full-length, glass showcase top. Not surprisingly, it was hugely heavy. We also had a curious, wardrobe-shaped, upright changing room made for customers wanting to try on the new Proban flameproof racing overalls. As it was unlit and felt like standing up in a coffin, even potential racing drivers were not brave enough to stay inside it for long.

Both items weighed so much that we had to use one of the Rice horse trailers, sold by the Sturgess Garage over the road, to carry it all. There was also all the stock for ten days in London to transport, so our convoy comprised a Land Rover, the towed horsebox and my work Mini van. For economy accommodation we had rented a rather basic flat near Olympia, although we were only in it for brief sleeps.

The Robin Sturgess Accessories stand was one of the smallest in the show, but we were betting on big sales of the new wood rim and leather bound steering wheels and had bought in plenty of stock. We also had a deal with the actual suppliers, Les Leston, who had the largest stand on the far side of the hall.

All the steering wheel rims were 15-in flat ones, supplied separately from the cast alloy bosses. They were mainly for Minis, Ford Anglias and Cortinas, Triumph Heralds and Spitfires, but of course they had to be assembled for each customer and as soon as the show opened we were hard at work assembling wheels at around £7 a time. By the evening peak we were plucking the nearest banknotes from eager hands and screwing wheels together as fast as our weary fingers would allow.

As stock ran out we had to make a nifty sprint across the hall to Les Leston for more wheels. All this, often with someone crammed into our upright coffin wardrobe trying on flameproof underwear was a multi-tasking challenge. Neighbouring exhibitors included Downton Engineering, with their hot cylinder heads, Westover driving shoes and Allard, demonstrating their impressive tubular dragster for order on the stand. Immediately next door was *Autocar* magazine, still very much with us in 2020 and Duckhams Oils, back then launching their green Q20-50 motor oil.

As the show closed each evening, we cleared out the little wooden till of all the cash – no credit cards in those days – and headed out on the town with the proceeds. Usually there was a small surplus to be banked, except for the Saturday night, spent in the West End at Danny La Rue's Club. Happy days!

The firm's Mini van, with a black and white chequered roof, was okay, but not very macho, even with the weekend kit of a lightweight mattress installed in the back. My mother believed it was to absorb the noisy, echoing vibrations of an empty van at weekends and I suppose it did in a way.

My income was growing tidily by then and having speedy aspirations, I saw a just affordable, but well-used 1340cc Cosworth Lotus Super 7 advertised the other side of Canterbury. Rather rashly, I took a rail journey to see the car and fell for it on the spot. The equally rash owner was prepared to accept my cheque. So I drove it back through central London, both in the dark and during a thunderstorm. Water came in everywhere – up through the floor and down through the dashboard. Hisses and sparks flared around the tiny cabin and I arrived home soaked and exhausted.

Beside the incredible acceleration the Lotus offered, another benefit for the more amorous driver was that the handbrake was halfway down the passenger footwell, just above the passenger's knees. Whether this was a plus or minus in the relationship stakes rather depended on the companion. I loved the car deeply, but it had many disadvantages and this Spartan driving experience was not to last, even with the only useable extra accessory – a cushion for the driver. I sold the Lotus to a Swedish chap who had designs on it for ice racing. He paid me on the ramp of the car ferry in Harwich, in cash – and later sent me a photo of it sitting on studded tyres, primed for racing on a frozen lake.

THREE

GADGETS (AND MINIS) GALORE

L IFE IN THE SHOP WAS INCREASINGLY INTERESTING, AS the stock inventory overflowed everywhere. Big bore silencers ranged around the upstairs bathroom; the bath was full of lamp brackets; fog and spotlights occupied the front bedroom and the back bedroom was stacked with steering wheels. Stretching up the stairs were boxes of racing boots on every step. Life was also more than 'interesting' in another way, as the staff and I had fallen in love and we soon became engaged.

We were just getting underway with our wholesale motor accessory activities and I realised that while owner-occupied motor accessory shops were beginning to open in all corners of the country, most of them didn't know how to obtain many of the newly popular or specialised products, but with some detective work and without Google or Internet, we did.

I started to undertake three-day explorations in the Minivan to undersupplied areas, such as East Anglia, Devon, Cornwall, Northumberland and Wales. On arrival at each new location I would look for the nearest phone box. In those days there was always a Yellow Pages on the shelf inside, so naughtily ripping out the page covering car accessory shops enabled me to make a plan of action for each area. (Remember, the Internet and Google were 30 years in the future!)

My physique developed accordingly as I staggered into each shop carrying three large, heavy suitcases, full of samples. Curiosity over the contents always gained me a hearing, decent orders to be sent on and thus a sizeable, although far-flung, clientele evolved.

On one pre-seasonal trip to North Wales I was also selling a new range of very smart, Harry Moss Austi roof racks and I had a brand new demonstration model clamped to the roof of the van. By the third day of the trip I had taken plenty of orders, but all on monthly credit accounts, as was normal in those days and I had spent my cash reserves on bed and breakfasts, meals out and petrol. I was therefore virtually penniless when I realised that having a nearly empty tank and no cash, while being somewhere near Llandudno, left me unable to get home. (No credit or debit cards in 1967 and my last cheque had gone.)

The only option was to try and sell the very handsome demonstration roof rack and luckily a filling station soon came into view. I managed to persuade the proprietor that he needed to start selling roof racks. Magically, the demo rack was swapped for five gallons of Esso and I just made it back to Leicester.

On another trip to North Wales, by 7pm I was finding all the B&Bs had their 'No Vacancies' signs up, but then I spotted a large board reading 'Bodysgallen Hall Hotel', pointing to a far-distant edifice up a long drive. I decided to hang the cost and parked my Minivan on the vast gravel drive outside the imposingly studded, but closed, oak front door.

Pulling on the iron lever bell eventually produced an impressively uniformed butler, who took one look at my scruffy, chequered roof van and frowningly told me: "We don't take commercials here Sir." It needed my now best persuasive salesman's skills to gain admission – this only on condition that I parked in the servants' car park. However, I had finally managed a night of luxury – strangely finding myself the novelty guest amidst a group of rich American tourists also staying overnight.

Before long, we were supplying most of our local garages and car dealers with their steering wheel requirements, as well as Cibié auxiliary lights, Maserati air horns and much Mini equipment. We were now wholesalers as well as retailers, with exclusive deals guaranteeing us East Midlands' exclusivity for some of the more specialised suppliers.

My 2% of the turnover was starting to become a problem though, not least because it didn't help in convincing building societies to provide a mortgage for an eventual marital home. My boss Robin and I then held a crucial and beery meeting in a local pub. This left me with 10% of the company, a decent guaranteed salary and – the best bit – a significantly larger commission on total sales.

By now there was a huge number of accessories available, so my next company car, a Mini of course, boasted every single product on the market bolted or stuck onto it like a mobile Christmas tree. Starting with a full-width, moulded dashboard bulging with instruments, we added racing seats, a special front grille bristling with lights and every other product in the range. *The Leicester Mercury* borrowed the car for a road test in February 1968 and made it the subject of a full-page feature article. It wasn't very fast though – due to the weight of all the paraphernalia it was carrying.

Whilst the firm's car was fine, I often got carried away by ads in car magazines (I still do) and spotted a Mini advertised by John Aley Racing, based in Slawston, Cambridge. John was well known in motorsport circles and was also the first manufacturer of tubular rollover bars and cages for race and rally cars. The car he was selling, he said, had a few minor modifications and a little competition history. He was a very persuasive salesman and rather foolishly I actually bought it over the 'phone, sending him a cheque to secure it and getting dropped off a week later to collect it. It was BMC Old English White, complete with hubcaps and carpets and looked fairly normal. However, hanging from the choke knob was a bunch of race scrutineering inspection tickets, including Silverstone, Brands Hatch, Oulton Park and the notorious Nurburgring in Germany.

The heater had been removed to save weight and it had Perspex windows. It was fitted with a racing clutch, which was either in or out, so you couldn't drive it gently or very smoothly and it also had rock-hard racing shock absorbers, so it felt like driving a brick. To cap it all, the race-prepared engine had a very high-lift camshaft, which meant that while at less than 3,000 revs it was very sluggish, from then on the power came in explosively. To use it as a normal road-going commuter car necessitated every ounce of concentration, as well as much warm clothing. It did shake a lot as well, very appropriate, as the Beach Boys had just topped the 1966 charts with *Good Vibrations*.

Very soon the bank manager was starting to worry me and I had to sell the car fast, but I wasn't really sorry. However, my local adverts were not pulling in the punters, until one day a surprising call from a local nursing home revealed that two of their nurses (who were all nuns) had seen my advert and were interested. They duly turned up in full nuns' regalia, including winged, triangular wimples and I drove them very carefully on a short and cautious demonstration run round the block. "Nice little car," they said and I grabbed their offer, as the bank manager was pressing. On collection two days later, the last I saw of it they were driving jerkily off up the road in kangaroo hops with their wimples wagging well. I shall have my fingers crossed when the Pearly Gates come into view.

By now the Mini craze was enormous and a popular major modification was to cut off all the front bodywork forward of the windscreen and replace it with a full, lift-off fibreglass front end. The cars were strong enough to handle this; it improved engine accessibility and saved a lot of weight.

Time moved on, but rather fast, as now, in 1968, I had become both a married man and a home-owner and we had recruited a full time shop manager, Bob Jones, who knew a lot more about cars than my wife did and she had other priorities by that time anyway. The fibreglass Mini front ends were the crunch point: where to store them? Clearly we had to move. The little shop at 169 Walnut St had at least got us started.

In February 1968 we located a corner shop on a main road, Abbey Lane, in Leicester. It adjoined a small next-door terraced house and the two properties had a back yard, on which we constructed a small timber-framed warehouse. This meant we could keep in touch with car crazy customers and trends via the bigger accessory shop on the front, but we could also carry far more stock in the new warehouse at the back, as well as in the five-bedrooms above. Motor accessory fashions were changing all the time by then and soon we had a fully fitted out transit van covering the East Midlands with a full-time salesman.

That same year the London to Sydney endurance rally was held and won by Andrew Cowan in a Hillman Hunter, driving against such rally legends as Roger Clark and Paddy Hopkirk. During the Australian leg the motoring press made much of the collision dangers with stray kangaroos and the fact that the competing cars had to have special kangaroo protection bars fitted at the front. Amazingly, this triggered another craze and we needed to find a manufacturer to fabricate full-width, plastic-coated kangaroo bars to fit Minis, Cortinas and various other models. We must have sold hundreds before the craze died a death, but it was a good lesson in not reordering too many of anything!

Even then the buyer of a Bentley expected it to come fully equipped with wing mirrors, reversing lights and screenwash equipment. Lesser cars in those days lacked such luxuries however, so someone had to supply them all. Luckily we were by this time stocking 15 different types of wing mirror, including the pointed racing mirrors, as well as manual screenwash kits, reversing lights and before long, electrification kits as an extra to save pushing a plunger to work the screen washers.

These were the days when the Ford Cortina, 105E, Triumph Herald and BMC 1100s were very popular, as were the Austin

Healey Sprite and the Spitfire, but they all lacked most of the extras now considered basic necessities. Sportier customers also wanted oil coolers and full-width lamp brackets to take three or four lamps. Smiths industries and Silverline then introduced stick-on, rear-screen heaters, which sold very quickly in the winter and we had half a bedroom full of stock. Very few car manufacturers fitted reversing lights or car alarms. The Selmar alarm was a top seller and of course, who didn't want a smart dashboard-mounted car compass on a suction cup to supplement their map-reading skills?

The Government was unwittingly of great service to the accessory trade with some most welcome legislation. Starting with safety belts having to be Kitemark approved from 1962, the window of opportunity made a compulsory fitment from 1968 quite wonderful before the wearing of belts was mandated in 1983.

It was another happy day when the first high level brake warning lights appeared. We had a good few years until they became compulsory, but they were never an easy job to fit. Reflective number plates were legalised and launched in 1970, but the trade had three clear years of profit from aftermarket sales until car dealers had to fit them on new car sales in 1973.

Probably the best was children's safety seats. Through 1960 what little was available didn't even have to be anchored to anything and they must have been about as much use in a crash as a catapult. The aftermarket then had a completely clear run starting with proper products by Britax, Jeenay and Kangol in 1962, but actually putting a child in them was not legally enforced until 2006 using the ISO fix anchorages built into all cars. Children's safety seats though were the toughest item of all for the motoring family man to install. Much drilling of floor panels and door pillars was required, as well as access under the car. It was certainly never wise to attempt the job with impressionable children in earshot, as the air turned blue.

The police were now beginning to deploy radar speed traps and Invicta Plastics in Oadby, Leicester, (makers of Master Mind, the 1972 Game of the Year) had started producing a product called the Radatetec. This was powered by two small torch batteries and clipped onto the sun visor, and purported to give you plenty of warning. As it was a local firm, we supported them and sold quite a few, although we never had the slightest evidence that it actually worked. Still, it gave a most reassuring buzzing noise while switched on.

Bearing in mid that at that time our invoices were all being handwritten on triple-layer carbon paper machines, it was a challenge when decimalisation came in on 15 February 1971. In fact everyone seemed to get used to it fairly quickly, although like others, we didn't resist the temptation to round things up a little for simplicity's sake.

The Mini was as popular as ever, especially when the Mini Cooper hit the market and the extra wide, reverse rim wheels became even more desirable, while Rostyle wheels for the Ford range became a big seller. A year or two later, the Mini Cooper S came equipped with much wider and stronger wheels, which also were perforated with one-inch holes around the inside of the rim to improve airflow for better brake cooling. While these looked very sporty, they were also very expensive and in short supply. I wonder who it was who had the idea of selling pretend ventilation holes as one-inch black adhesive dots to stick all around the inside rim of the ordinary cream-coloured Mini wheels? They didn't do a lot for brake cooling, but they were only fours shillings a packet and looked really snazzy.

11 MINIS

My own first few Minis, of the ten I have owned over the years, were 848cc, although often with various engine modifications. But then came the first really hot one, a 1071cc Cooper S, already souped up by its first owner. It was a revelation and I started entering a fair few local rallies run by Leicestershire Car Club and the Kirkby Mallory Car Club.

Interestingly, on my very first rally, the car in front of me was driven by Bob Gerard from Leicestershire. He was Britain's first Grand Prix racing driver of the 1940s and '50s and this was his last ever competitive event.

Britain's top international rally driver Roger Clark turned up for one event in a factory-sponsored Ford Capri, considered somewhat unsportsmanlike by the rest of us. All the rallies were run through the middle of the night on open public roads and with timed sections. Fastest was best (of course now no longer legal). Secrets of some factory team modifications leaked out. I fitted a brake light cutout switch on my car, very useful on night stages if being too closely tailgated by the following driver relying on my brake lights. So when the navigator said "hairpin left coming up" I just flicked off the brake lights and tempted the driver following too close behind to end up in the hedge.

Autocross racing had become very popular amongst the motor clubs. A large field was marked out as a track and two cars at a time left the start for two flat-out laps on slippery grass, but you couldn't go too mad as most of us needed the cars to go to work. After a prizeless season, I decided that a Mini Moke would be ideal. They were so light that you could lift the back off the ground by grasping the tubular rear bumper. One winter was spent installing a Cooper S engine, a rollover cage and a special Bostrom driver's seat. We had at the time acquired the agency for these very sophisticated lorry seats, which incorporated a hydraulic mechanism for the truck driver, so going over any severe bumps the seat automatically compensated. The first autocross and the first big bump hit at speed in the field shot my crash-helmeted head upwards into the rollover hoop, which promptly plunged me down into the seat, then repeated the process – not a success.

To make matters worse, Players' Cigarettes had a similar Moke idea. Not only did they sponsor the whole next season national Autocross racing with The Players No. 6 Autocross Championship, but they also themselves entered a team of modified Mini Mokes in branded colours, which were even faster than mine! This was

NOT JUST FURRY DICE...

thought by all to be a bit 'off'.

My last Mini was a beautiful, silver 970cc Cooper S with black Cooper 'rose-petal' wheels – very rare now. I wanted to see it on track, but didn't have the higher level of RAC competition licence, so Robin Sturgess gamely drove it for me, unfortunately with little success, at Silverstone. This was his last competitive drive.

BIG GAME CHANGERS

THERE'S ALWAYS A BIG BUZZ TO MAKING A SALE, especially when getting a new range through to a new customer. My huge, heavy leather suitcases for samples, having been dumped on the floor of a freshly found shop, meant I was never ejected, as curiosity always got the better of the proprietor and once we got started there were always a few products that appealed. I never wrote the orders down on a formal order pad in front of the customer in case the list, as it got longer, frightened the proprietor. Instead I used various scraps of paper and transcribed these at night over dinner, wherever I happened to be staying, on one of our proper internal order forms.

Sometimes a particularly important line or regular profitable repeating range, such as a huge variety of key fobs on a display stand, or a new range of wiper blades, was really important to get established. In these cases I had a special technique. The secret was to present six or seven items I knew would be rejected, start to look visibly wretched, but coming to the eighth – and key – product, hit the customer with a hard sell that usually succeeded in gaining a YES out of sympathy.

Removing a car's hefty air filter/silencer assembly grew popular for a noisier under the bonnet airflow (to impress the passenger) so naturally the sale of ram-pipes and pancake-style air filters became a firm favourite, to supplement the racket from the big bore exhaust silencers.

Among the suppliers was a London firm called Speedwell, producing a variety of go-faster equipment and we acquired the East Midlands distribution rights. The chairman of Speedwell was Graham Hill, who by late 1968 already had 12 Formula One wins under his belt and had achieved Motor sport's Triple Crown, meaning that in one year he had won the Monaco Grand Prix, the Le Mans 24 Hours and the Indianapolis 500. As we were valued customers of Speedwell I managed to persuade Graham to drive up to Leicester for a trade open day at our little premises and he was wonderful company, spending nearly four hours chatting with our customers. Considering that he also won the British Grand Prix that summer it really helped to put us on the map.

We had persuaded all our suppliers to buy supporting advertising in a double page spread in *The Leicester Mercury* to celebrate the special day, but the paper refused to send a photographer, or do a write up, as they said, "It will impinge on our editorial integrity, as you are an advertiser, but if an outside disturbance is caused such as a traffic jam, that will count as news and we will cover it"!

Back in the shop, space required for carrying stock was again becoming a major problem, as the lightweight fibreglass body sections for many of the saloon cars being used for motorsport were extremely bulky. By the early 1970s roof racks were becoming quite sophisticated and easy to fit, but they took up a lot of room and we sold huge quantities, so along with the continued growth of big bore silencers and various clothing lines, our small warehouse and the bedrooms were bursting at the seams. We had to think about moving – again.

My own time was increasingly taken up with sourcing, buying and running the business, so we recruited a local man as our travelling rep, to take over and expand the accounts I had set up and to open new ones. One of my existing customers was in deepest central Wales in Newtown, Powys. It was the only accessory shop across vast areas of sheep country and I could only justify visiting annually in the spring to put his summer requirements 'in the bag' and show him any new products. I was slow on the uptake to notice that our new rep's petrol bills were escalating and that this very rural, isolated customer was receiving a visit every two weeks – and he wasn't even a very good payer. Of course the answer lay in female form, so the romance was swiftly curtailed, but I allowed the randy rep to keep his job!

One new product was the sunroof, but those installations made by leading manufacturers such as a proper Webasto sliding roof could only be fitted by specialists at huge expense. But before long an enterprising supplier started offering DIY sunroofs in a box. The kit comprised the glass, lots of rubber seals, various parts and pages of very optimistic instructions. The intrepid customer merely needed some tinsnips, (or a can opener) and a great deal of courage – plus, for the ham-fisted, a waterproof hat.

As luck would have it, suitable warehouse premises became vacant only two doors up the road on the same side, giving us at least four times the floor space. We decided to keep the original Robin Sturgess shop, as it was trading well, but to create a new trading name for the wholesale motor factoring operation. We called ourselves RSA Factors Ltd, and started proper motor factor wholesale trading out of 303 Abbey Lane, leaving the shop still at 307/309.

As RSA we could now focus on spreading our net wider and we passed on the van delivery responsibility to a Cambridge firm, who put two vans on the road full time, exclusively dedicated to our range of products and buying their entire stock from us. We were by now supplying most of the east of the country, right up to the coast with our specialist range, as well as the far-flung areas I had set up many years before, where we had retained specialist outlets and which now included parts of Northumberland. I had a

1750 Austin Maxi at the time and whenever I was due to visit our good customer in Tynemouth he always wanted me to fold down the seats and carry 20 Rostyle steel wheels for Fords in the car up to him to save paying carriage. These were extremely heavy, so the car sat solid on the bump stops and was scarcely driveable, but I never denied him his saving.

We had added the Isle of Man, Wales and the Channel Islands, all of which I visited twice a year, since no one else did. Part of our policy was to try and confirm exclusive area distributorships, particularly for the more specialised ranges, such as Cibié rally lighting and Les Leston's huge range. Added to Paddy Hopkirk products and Yazaki instruments and with a few other exclusives, we had also started to really tie up the East Midlands.

A good handful of customers had begun to enjoy the experience of coming to visit us from some distance. These included one shop owner who twice a year drove over from Belfast and having browsed our stock shelves, spotted anything he might have missed in terms of new products and then always purchased a Rice Trailer Horsebox from the Sturgess depot and filled it to the roof with our goodies for the journey home.

We found a way to further encourage visiting by using several advantages with the new premises. One was the fact that we backed onto Hoskins Brewery, which produced a particularly good bitter. Any visiting customers who spent over £100 were treated to as much beer as they could drink. To carry it all we used two tall, white enamel jugs, which we took across the road and filled from the brewery tanks. This also contributed to relaxing staff tea breaks.

The second benefit from the move was that we had acquired a partially flat roof, accessed from an upstairs door. Having installed a large greenhouse on it with a barbecue inside, we recruited a local lady as our lunchtime cook and offered a full-scale fry up to trade customers who had spent well and travelled a long distance. What could be better for our loyal trade customers in the summer than a big fry up, a couple of pints and a sprawl on the rooftop deckchair before driving home?

The word soon spread. Our range was starting to expand. We were now offering a wide range of electronic in-car entertainment, such as Harry Moss radios, combined radio and cassette players and eight-track stereos, plus fancy speaker sets and a range of handheld tuning equipment from Crypton and others. The DIY market was now starting to really go places and it was difficult to drive round any residential area at the weekend without spotting lots of cars up on car ramps with their owners carrying out oil changes, adjusting carburettors, or doing basic servicing like changing sparking plugs.

Selling successfully was a huge buzz, but the buying was just as important and by this stage suppliers and manufacturers were knocking on our door knowing that our unusual distribution pattern would get them into a plethora of outlets. In the buying office my own chair was substantial and comfortable, but although the one on the other side of the desk looked okay, it had a faulty adjustment mechanism and would sometimes tilt alarmingly backwards. It was also a lot lower than mine. I must confess that sometimes sales reps became a little discomfited and did a decent deal just to escape.

On one occasion a rather cocky salesman was selling a small in-car aerosol fire extinguisher and was very keen to push the non-toxic benefits of the liquid propellant gas. For some reason he felt it necessary to claim the extinguishing liquid was drinkable and squirted some of it into a disposable plastic cup from which he had been drinking coffee. He then swigged it all down and put the cup on my desk, but still left without getting an order. A few minutes later, after he had driven away, I spotted a horrible mark burnt through the top of my desk – plus a bottomless coffee cup. I never saw him again.

Enthusiastic ownership also called for guidance – hence a huge boom in workshop manuals – and soon we found ourselves becoming booksellers, supplied by publishers such as Olyslager, Autobooks and Haynes.

Hand tools of every sort proliferated, especially socket sets from Draper and Kamasa. Car ramps were vital products, although very difficult to handle. The rally boys, or mostly more correctly the pretend rally boys, were getting ever more serious with replacement coil springs and suspension lowering kits and even more sophisticated rally seats. Remember, safety belts were still not compulsory yet, just a profitable extra.

Suddenly everyone wanted 'Tyre Dressers', a waxy coloured pencil in silver, white, or gold to emphasise the raised wording on the sidewalls of tyres. I doubt if even a top psychologist could explain why?

We were starting to move for the first time into the lucrative car care-chemical market, distributing such products as WD40 and underseal. It is extraordinary to think that in those days basic factory rustproofing of cars was hardly done at all. A few factory coats of paint was normal, but little else, with the only DIY rustproofing being brush-on, rubberized underseal – another good reason to buy some car ramps.

We were now getting into hosting twice-yearly 'trade evenings' at a nearby hotel, where our shop owning customers would be invited for a buffet and drinks and our keenest suppliers were invited to set up displays of their latest products for display, as well as paying for all the hospitality. After consuming enough beer the customers always gave us a decent order.

In April 1973 the Government introduced VAT. In some ways this was not easy, as we had no computerised invoicing, but at least it was set at 10%, which wasn't too hard to work out. A big innovation was our first electronic calculator, a Sharp, costing exactly £200 and operating from the mains electricity with a cable as thick as a pencil, but it was a huge help.

We had been publishing a quarterly trade discount catalogue, listing our full range of merchandise for some years. It had started fairly simply as an aide-memoire, but had now grown into a full-scale product directory running to 40 sides of paper with 12 sides of advertising from suppliers. It listed absolutely everything we supplied, with all the car model variations, retail and trade prices. The RSA catalogue had become something of a bible for our specialist trade suppliers and customers, even though we had never supplied 'spare parts' as such and just stuck to the more rarefied part of the after market.

The more obvious an accessory the more likely it would become a popular fad and you can't get more visible than a wing attached to the boot lid or an air dam/spoiler as wide as the car under the front bumper. Both products were pioneered by Richard Grant Motor Accessories, made in black polypropylene and before long were available for a wide range of cars, as all the bodywork shapes were of course different. The front facing products were simply copying the American Transam racers and were mainly cosmetic, but some of the rear 'wings' had a measurable aerodynamic effect. Grant's testing in the famous wind tunnel at MIRA showed the rear wheels on a standard Ford Sierra starting to lift off the ground at 100mph (so a worthwhile extra!) but mostly the black full-width wings on the boot lid were there for their 'bird-pulling' powers.

Very few products remained in constant, steady demand for all of the 30 golden years of the motor accessory business, but rubber floor mats were always selling. The market leader was Cannon, always first with the correctly shaped ones to fit the floor of any popular new car models and always in those days, in any colour, as long as it was black (apologies to Henry Ford).

As 1974 approached we heard a lot about a new firm in Coventry called GKN Spa Factors, who had opened a cash and carry warehouse for the motor trade. This had not been a concern until I went over there on a spying mission and found that among other items they were stocking much of the range we were carrying and as their prices were strictly cash they were worryingly competitive. At the same time our catalogue was getting very time consuming and maintaining monthly accounts needing very strict credit control was becoming difficult. We were also running out of space – yet again. We didn't just need to move, we needed to move our game – completely.

FIVE

WELL AND TRULY MOTORING

ABRAND NEW LEICESTER WAREHOUSE DEVELOPMENT had just been completed, enlarging the existing Freemen's Common trading estate on the edge of the city centre. One of the units of 12,000 square feet was located immediately opposite a major branch of Replacement Services Ltd, conveniently the county's biggest trade car parts supplier.

Renting was not in the Sturgess DNA, but selling the Abbey Lane freehold premises was a big boost, so we went for it. A vast amount of proper warehouse racking was bought, partitioned offices put up, a local carpenter constructed two wooden checkouts and we also bought our first, secondhand, forklift truck. We were now a fully-fledged cash and carry, RSA Factors C&C, but strictly trade. Additionally of course, now having no shop of our own stopped our customers complaining about unfair competition.

Moving from a mixture of stock stacked on the floor and spread across bedrooms in our previous modest premises, to a huge, racked out floor area now left plenty of space for further new product ranges. We had effectively gone from being a little corner shop to a proper hypermarket. Car care chemicals were always going to be the big one and now we could well and truly motor.

From Holts we had Duplicolor aerosol spray paints and touch-up bottles, which involved hundreds of colours, in addition to supplying special racking for our stockists. The Holts range of liquid and paste products included major brands like Gun-Gum exhaust repair stuff, Radweld, Turtle Wax and Molyslip oil additive.

STP oil additive, which I had doubted in the early days at Walnut Street, was now selling like crazy, with cases of 24 flying out, aptly proving the power of a brand, since few questioned the product claims.

It was a revelation to see our sales figures shoot up as other major brands came on board and at last we had room to carry a range of tow bars from Witter, which took us into the caravan accessory market.

Our clothing range expanded dramatically, as well as number plate kits and stick-on number plates, a nightmare at stocktaking time, counting all the digits in stock. Another one was leather key fobs, all bearing different makers' badges – around 100. It was always a surprise when doing the monthly order to find that there were many more Ferraris on the road than Fords!

A hugely popular product was the car alarm, the best seller being the Selmar, but as a DIY fit it did demand concentration and some rewiring under the bonnet. I fitted a demonstration unit to my wife's Austin 1300 estate, even though the car was due to be changed before long. At that time we lived in a village on top of a hill, Thorpe Satchville, near Melton Mowbray, where there is a long run down the hill to the next village. A friend was persuaded to buy the Austin and he and his wife came over to collect. They sped off in it, only to suffer a total brake failure as they shot down the hill through the next village and came to rest, brakeless, halfway up the other side, somewhat shaken. My fault, as when fitting the alarm I had accidentally put a screw through a panel, behind which ran the hydraulic brake-pipe. Brake fluid had been slowly leaking out for a month. I generously paid to have it repaired – and we are still friends.

The product needing the most space of all was the DIY workshop manual. Haynes had become pre-eminent as the other publishers fell by the wayside and having more than 100 titles, the manuals were a vital part of any shop's offering. We carried the lot, plus regular new titles. We received a weekly delivery via their own van from the publishers in Sparkford just to keep up with demand, as well as carrying the display racks for the stores to maximise sales.

The women's cosmetics and car care chemicals markets have much in common. Their products can improve your looks, cover up blemishes, do a bit of touching up and enhance the body. Often the aspiration is greater than the reality, so the really caring motorist could colour the exhaust manifold with Sperex heatproof paint, spray tint the windows, repel rain from the windscreen with Rainex and complete the makeover with Mother's Wax, Naval Jelly and even the intriguingly named Grundy's Petroids, which must have helped somewhere?

Now came the time of the rear screen visor. These big black, full width, multi-slatted visors copied the glamorous rear-engined Lamborghini Miura and the 1980 Lotus Esprit. The function was to enhance rear engine cooling behind the driver, but they also stopped the car behind easily seeing in and for the owner visibility wasn't impaired too much. Fixing such items onto a normal car did absolutely nothing useful, but they looked really macho and soon became available for most makes of car, even of course Minis! Luckily in those days rear screen wipers were almost unheard of, as that really would have been a problem, but hats off to Autoplas who made them – and a lot of money for the trade.

Stock control was becoming a real issue, with products like badges, stickers and gear knobs each having 50 or 60 different car manufacturers' logos in each range and we were starting to struggle, especially at checkout. Everything was recorded in writing on a humble stock card and counted going round the racks on a rotating weekly basis, then checked in the office, with a written order posted off to the supplier. Scanning and barcodes were still years away. At checkout, everything depended on the hand-applied price tag on the product, a list by the tills, or the memory of the checkout person, a considerable test of efficiency, with all those product lines from more than 150 different suppliers.

Always keen to innovate, we began planning our famous 'trade days' to bring in new customers with special offers, staying open twice a week until 9pm. We were now ready to try a big 'hook' to guarantee the best turnout. Bunny Girls were the first one. A deal with the Playboy Club in Mayfair resulted in two 'Bunnies', complete with ears, tails and high heels, posing for pictures with the punters. They were a massive success. A few months later, the next trade day was with Penthouse Pets – even raunchier than the Bunnies – and as the word got round, hard headed garage owners now started coming in, not usually with their wives.

Now it was time to get more respectable, so Stirling Moss agreed to attend our next trade day. After much haggling over the fee, he arrived at Leicester Station, on 9 December 1979, where I met him in my Rover 3500 SD1. This was my company car, bought from Sturgess stock, in a factory special edition colour scheme of vivid lime green with gold wheels. I'm not sure if our celebrity was impressed, but not many people have driven the most famous racing driver in the world from Leicester station to Freemen's Common. He didn't comment on my driving skills, but he did play Scalextric model car racing both against the customers' children and the grown-ups, some of whom could then boast they had beaten Stirling Moss on the track.

Once again running out of space, we now constructed a mezzanine floor covering a third of the downstairs floor area, which was allowable without adding to the rateable value. The only trouble was that it increased stock losses due to theft. Even downstairs it was a problem, with narrow aisles and high racks making shoplifting a cinch. A boxed crash helmet could easily conceal 20 sparking plugs.

Crash helmets were always a good stock line, particularly as the British Standard Kitemark grew ever more stringent. Customers had to keep upgrading to remain legal for motor racing. The original shape of an open face crash helmet was gradually losing popularity in favour of the full-face helmet with just the eye aperture and about this time we had advertised for a warehouse trainee. A young scooter-riding hopeful entered my office still wearing his full-face crash helmet. Flipping up his visor, he sat down waiting for the interview to start. Instead he was at the receiving end of a two-word instruction to leave the premises.

One of the most contradictory crazes involved the car's ride height. Following the hot-rod fad in America, 'jack-up kits' became popular to make the vehicles look higher and more dominant, only to do an about turn a few years later when the 'low-rider' look became fashionable and we had to carry suspension lowering kits! Neither would currently meet transport legislation, nor did either improve cornering characteristics, but hey, the customer is always right ...

The most significant trend developing was in motor trade cash and carry warehouses covering vast floor areas. Competitors Gordon Spice were now up to three units, GKN Spa Factors four units and Maccess five units. Regor in Manchester had a mammoth 'shed', which at 40,000 square feet, was the biggest anywhere. Whilst we had been in at the start we were now on our own and the competition was getting fiercer and nearer. We started to think, "What now?" Things were moving fast and suddenly it transpired that Peter Unwin, originally of the Kettering Tyres empire and now the founder of the very first GKN Spa cash and carry had joined forces with racing driver Gordon Spice's firm. They then approached us offering a merger, or what was effectively a takeover, joining forces in order to improve our joint buying power and benefit from other economies of scale.

Robin Sturgess had personally been almost totally in the background of day-to-day RSA activity for around 17 years and he now needed to devote even more time to the burgeoning car franchises within the family group. For him, this all came at the right time, but it left me holding the baby. In most ways it made good economic sense for him and for Spice, but for me, not so good. Having been a minority shareholder before, my share was now further diluted. My income had always been a salary, plus a large sales commission, but now my safety net was less secure; there were many new directors and shareholders, but no Robin. So the Spice/RSA Group became the UK's latest and second largest player in the C&C distribution stakes with six warehouses.

Just as pressure on space was intensifying, the next-door warehouse fell vacant, so our new company immediately took on the lease, knocked two huge access doors through the intervening wall and almost overnight we had doubled our floor space to 24,000 sq ft. After the greenhouse rooftop experience at Abbey Lane, our regulars had been greatly missing their fry-ups, so with a lot more floor space, we erected a second, smaller mezzanine floor, creating a canteen to feed our customers, staff and the many visiting reps. This worked well, as we could also provide in-house hospitality for our trade days.

Whilst selling successfully was always vital, the buying was just as important and by this stage suppliers and manufacturers were knocking on our door knowing that our unusual distribution pattern would get them into a plethora of little-known outlets. Metal petrol cans had always been a big seller, but now arrived red plastic versions from Bell Products who also introduced plastic oil drainer cans. These were a runaway success that saved many an oil-stained driveway.

As car ownership grew, so did car theft and few cars had much factory fitted security. The Krooklock steering wheel to pedal lock, introduced by Brown Brothers, was the first and early bestseller, followed by various gear lever and handbrake locks. Some years later came the cross steering wheel Metro Lock, eventually the most popular physical protection and market leader for many years. As alloy wheels became ever more popular, especially the very handsome Wolfrace wheels, they were soon being stolen, with cars left propped on bricks, so locking wheel nuts soon became a vital extra. The most popular were the Carflow locknuts, a wonderful new source of profit for the shops, as alloy wheels proliferated and few car manufacturers fitted wheel locks as standard.

Winter was a good season for the trade before the outlets for aerosol de-icers became widespread and we received literally a long lorry load of 30 pallets every September, awaiting the first frosts, when the whole lot would be gone in days. Anti-freeze was still necessary, as few carmakers then included year-round radiator fluids. As winter deepened, battery jump lead sets were a very steady mover through the shops, as was a great variety of 12-volt battery chargers. Only classic cars and some supercars really need them nowadays, but in those days Davenset and Crypton dominated this lucrative market sector.

The customising craze was developing fast, based on American trends, some of which translated well to our home market. Such unnecessary products as 'dagger dipsticks' and huge, Bigfoot accelerator extensions started to move and we were beginning to see a demand for Thrush Mufflers. These American-style, chrome-plated exhaust pipes running beside the doorsill were completely inappropriate for the UK's small cars, but bestowed masses of street cred.

WAY OUT WEST

Having met David Riswick of the American parts importers John Woolfe Racing, I was given the chance to accompany him to Las Vegas for the huge international trade exhibition held by SEMA (Speciality Equipment Manufacturers' Association) to make contacts and to do some buying across the latest gadget lines, after surveying the latest car fashion fads before they crossed the ocean.

It was now October 1977 and my co-directors in the whole group were keen for me to go on the group's behalf. But I had just suffered a great blow. My wife, dear Nollie, died from cancer, aged 33 and our girls were six and eight. I had the unimaginable task of breaking the news to them, neither of them being aware how ill she really had been. Thanks to wonderful family support, it was decided that I should nevertheless make the vital American trip.

David then pointed out that the very first Concorde flights into Washington were imminent. If I wanted the right introductions at the show I would have to join him and since he was going that way I would have to go supersonic as well. My skills of salesmanship with the new board of directors were never more tested. The board reluctantly agreed and he and I crossed the Atlantic with BA in fine style, in three hours 20 minutes. I shall never forget the Captain's announcement soon after takeoff, "We are now over the Bristol Channel, travelling at 1,000 mph and beginning to accelerate". We arrived in Washington before we had left – and had even been offered Havana cigars, at 62,000ft high, after a lavish in-flight lunch.

This first trip to Las Vegas was a complete eye-opener. We were booked into the Hilton and like all the other hotel/casinos, the ground floor reception was surrounded by acres of slot machines and gaming tables. No windows on the ground floor and public clocks nowhere to be seen. At the first breakfast I was persuaded to buy a 'Keno' ticket by a lovely, barely-dressed lady in fishnet tights and she told me to watch the screens on the wall in case my lucky number came up. Five minutes later it did and I had won $500. That night I took a turn on the blackjack tables and there was a disturbance a few minutes later as someone took over the chair next to me, surrounded by a bevy of girls. It was Telly Savalas, TV's Kojak. He was betting $50 chips as opposed to my $5 bets. I bid him "Good Evening", but he just grunted and sucked his lolly stick.

With Dave as my mentor, a very worthwhile and interesting two days were spent cruising the gigantic show and placing orders before the flight back via Washington and thence by Concorde to Heathrow. The UK had just been plunged into a rare journalists' strike, so it struck me that a page or two on my trip, possibly entitled 'By Concorde to Las Vegas' might appeal to my local paper, *The Leicester Mercury* and it was, at £50 per page.

Soon after publication, I received a letter from lawyers acting for Dunlop Aerospace, who made Concorde's brakes. In my piece I had added a little to the drama of Concorde's takeoff by saying that "letting the power build up to a peak, the pilot released the brakes and we shot off up the runway". Evidently, the brakes had been facing overheating problems, with BA accusing Dunlop of substandard product. Dunlop in turn was accusing the airline pilots of causing their own problems by using the brakes to contain the power before opening the throttles, thereby burning them out. Somewhat embarrassed, I had to explain that I had rather over imagined the takeoff experience

On balance, the trip paid off and we were first in the field with a good array of weird add-ons, including direct sourcing for 'Mother's Wax' and the Thrush Muffler. This long, chromium-plated silencer surely became the most dangerous accessory ever imported, as the hot chrome pipes running by the doors burnt any bare legs very painfully. Health and Safety were thankfully many moons away.

The merger with Spice enabled us to enter the era of modern communications, with linked systems, meaning that across the seven-warehouse group, prices and discounts at the checkout could now all be the same. Although that sounds very normal and straightforward nowadays, it was anything but in the early '80s. To achieve this we had to rent a dedicated 24/7 'phone line to head office in Staines and then construct a small, sealed air-conditioned computer room to house the terminal the Leicester end of the line in case dust or vibration interfered with the operation of the computer. Even then we had 'outages' and a power cut was total disaster, with engineers from London having to be urgently dispatched.

One nice little earner was the tinted, anti-glare sun strip running across the top of the windscreen, in blue or green. It wasn't long before people started personalising them using white, stick-on number plate letters, so the driver and wife or girlfriend could proudly proclaim, in bold letters standing out from the tinted strip, 'David and Liz' either side of the screen.

Around 1975 the first and arguably 'most seen ever' accessory appeared – the famous Furry Dice – to hang on the rear-view mirror. The function or purpose has been lost in the mists of time, but who cared? They sold and delivered a huge profit margin. As respectable motor factors we hung our heads in embarrassment and stocked them, but we firmly rejected the parcel shelf favourite of 1979 – the 'Nodding Dog'. We had our standards!

Our next Trade Day needed a guest racing driver of some repute and retired Grand Prix driver Jackie Stewart, who had driven in 100 Grand Prix races, arrived for half a day, courtesy of the Ford Motor Company, some of whose more specialised items we were then handling.

My new board of directors now had real empire-building ambitions and had already opened in Cardiff and Bristol, in addition to a megastore over in east London, at Canning Town, just where the Olympic stadium was later built. The north of England beckoned and before long a warehouse in Sheffield, at 24,000 sq ft, the same size as the enlarged Leicester site, was taken on. In November 1978 we opened there with a big local fanfare.

In April 1973 the first fitted in-car telephones were introduced by Motorola and soon after actual handheld mobile phones appeared, but they were about as heavy as a brick, complete with a handle and a very long aerial mast. I was not an immediate early adopter because of the high cost and hopeless reception, but before long a well-heeled supplier who was having trouble finding his way to our premises telephoned us for help on his mobile and we talked him into our office as he followed our directions. This really was a first and a good dinner party tale to tell, but it was the 1980s before mobile 'phones became at all affordable and sat navs weren't around due to a lack of satellites.

By then staff numbers for Leicester and Sheffield combined numbered more than 40 and I was group-managing director for The Midlands and the North. The whole automobile aftermarket was by now booming. There were nearly 7,000 independent motor accessory shops, plus various shop chains expanding, not least of course being Halfords, which was now up to more than 300 shops. This made the total outlets for motor accessories nearly 8,000, the peak as it turned out. (42 years later it's down to less than 1000, plus Halfords).

Competition was rearing its head on all sides and margins were shrinking, but overall turnover was up and I had been voted a decent pay rise by the group board in London. A few months later, a top management board meeting was called at the country house home of one of the directors, at Virginia Water, in the heart of London's stockbroker belt. We covered a broad agenda during the morning session and my views were solicited on a number of topics. Among other subjects, we discussed staff appraisals in my northern section and my opinion was sought on pay rises or dismissals, where appropriate.

A little croquet was even played on the lawn at lunchtime, as white-coated waiters plied us with wine and refreshments. After lunch we returned to continue the meeting, which also involved further appraisals of senior staff and mine had been saved to the end. At that point I was handed an envelope and suddenly my colleagues left the room. I sat there on my own and opened it, finding that the letter basically declared me inefficient and no longer needed. I was deeply shocked, not least because I had recently received a letter 'patting me on the back', along with the notification of a pay rise. My immediate thought was that I now had two little daughters depending on me and I was out of work.

My erstwhile colleagues then re-entered the room and I protested, "But I have your letter in my briefcase giving me a pay rise only a few months ago for good service." They responded by telling me to get my lawyers to talk to theirs. In a daze I drove slowly off down the long, snaking drive, only to be blocked at the gates by one of the directors in a Porsche. He had taken a short cut across the grounds to head me off, then demanded that the 'well done', letter I had just referred to, be given back to them, since it was company property. Having parked his car across the gate he wouldn't let me leave until I handed the letter back. Still shell-shocked and under threat, I did so, which didn't help when negotiating my severance package.

Eventually, after 16 years from the start at Walnut Street, I came away with enough to keep my small family going for about three

Really? Sold a lot but never saw the result.

Richard Grant was king of the wings, air dams and spoilers business.

(Top) *Wolfrace wheels demmo car.*
(Bottom Left) *Barry Treacy "Mr Locking Wheel Nuts" with HRH the Duke of Kent.*

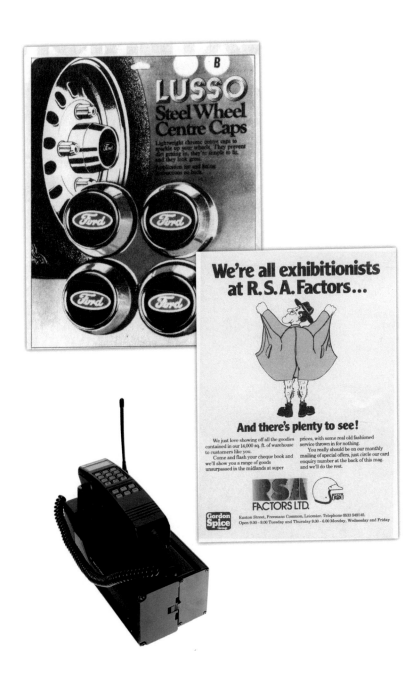

(Middle) *...and so there was!*
(Bottom) *Nifty "little" mobile.*

CUSTOM CORNER

It is a well known fact that the more flashy something is in the customizing market the better it sells; and what could be shinier or sexier than a pair of long deep chrome mufflers poking out from under the sills either side of a car. The lads love them and your potential market is all your customers with driving licences between the ages of 17yrs and 27yrs who have regular jobs and no marital ties and probably quite a lot of money to burn.

Side pipes are easy to fit and easy to stock — the normal problems associated with stocking exhaust systems don't apply. All you need is the side pipe kit and one of the semi universal hook-up kits and you are away. A lot of firms don't even bother with the hook-up kits and simply sell the customer the side pipes a piece of flexible exhaust tubing and link the whole thing together with a Y piece and a couple of step down adaptors, all available ex-stock at RSA.

There are a number of brand names in the side pipe business but the best known one in this country is undoubtedly Thrush. Thrush do basically three different price ranges of silencer and they are as follows:—

1. Phantoms — these are the least expensive end of the market.
2. Sidekicks — these are the original ones and are middle of the range in price with a thicker diameter and deeply louvred cover.

3. The Outsiders — these are the top end of the market and have a cast alloy shield and really handle the power from big engines effectively.

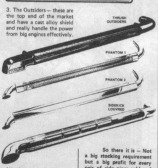

THRUSH OUTSIDERS
PHANTOM 1
PHANTOM 2
SIDEKICK LOUVRED

All of these three come in four different basic sizes —
50" fits Minis, Spridgets, Imps etc.
60" fits Escorts and Avenger sized cars.
70" are most suitable for Transit vans, Granadas, Jaguars etc.
80" which are only available for special order fit the long wheelbase vans and trucks.

So there it is — Not a big stocking requirement but a big profit for every pair of side pipes sold and every pair sold in your area is another pair for the custom fanatics to drool over and to want to buy themselves for their own "mean-machines".

Ask for the full colour multi-page Thrush Muffler catalogue — put a silencer or two in the window and wait for "fireworks".

The Thrush Mufflers came from travelling supersonic to Las Vegas trade shows.

Plenty of products...

(Top) *Someone had to be the chaperone.*

(Top) *The Metro Autolock was a top seller for years.*
(Bottom) *Ken Harris of Autoplas started the craze for rear window slats "a la Lamborghini."*

Early pre-trade Waxoyl advert – only cheques and postal orders accepted!

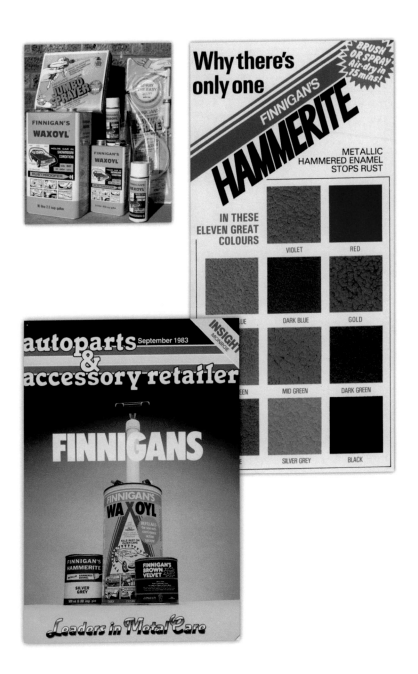

Relaunching the brands to the trade.

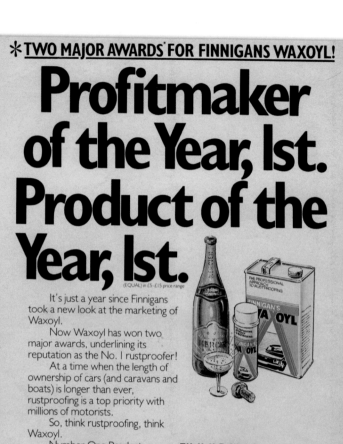
Success for Mitchell Marketing in first year after launch.

(Top) *The Backflash was a huge seller – nothing to do with the dress code of our sales ladies.*

Every now and then another new wonder product turns up. It promises more power. Or more mpg. Or longer engine life. Sometimes all three.

To no-one's great surprise, the response from the motor trade is usually pretty underwhelming. Which makes the run-away success of Slick 50 a real puzzle to the pundit.

performance improver that improves performance. From the trade we hear only reports of customers popping back to say how pleased they are with their Slick 50.

Of course we have had the odd trade complaint. It seems some of you couldn't get enough of it when we launched it.

Well, we're sorry about that. But Slick 50 just proved to be more popular with motorists than even we'd anticipated.

Fortunately, we're confident we can deliver anything you ask.

Which is just as well, because our £80,000 advertising campaign is still running in the national press.

THE MOST EXCITING AUTOMOTIVE PRODUCT SINCE THE NON-STICK FRYING PAN.

But then Slick 50 is a bit different from the average wonder product.

For a start, it really does deliver lasting benefits. It really can give motorists more power, more mpg and an engine that's more likely to serve them longer.

It works because it doesn't work like ordinary oil additives.

We've found a way of making PTFE, the stuff that makes non-stick pans non-stick, actually bond to all the moving metal surfaces of the engine.

It fills all the pits and valleys of the metal to give a permanent coating of PTFE. So instead of metal rubbing against metal, you get PTFE rubbing against PTFE. And that creates a lot less friction.

Already we've had hundreds of letters from motorists saying how amazed they are to find a

And we now have a gearbox treatment too!

Your usual supplier should have all the Slick 50 you need, both for engines and gearboxes.

But if you have any problems, call us direct at Mitchell Marketing, on Leicester (0533) 881522.

Slick 50 is one wonder product that won't stick on your shelves.

MITCHELL MARKETING

Mitchell Marketing, 140 Leicester Road, Wigston, Leicester LE8 1DU.

Our first ad to launch a hitherto unknown product to the UK trade.

(Top) *Getting slick on track.*
(Middle) *Roland Ratzenberger driving.*
(Bottom) *Mr and Mrs Sten Ahlberg with Harry Toms in Kensington.*

(Top) *Roger Clark in the car with no oil.* (Bottom) *One free with every seven packs?*

Paddock hospitality and errant motorists.

(Top) *Roger Clark interviewed with Metro 6R4 at Mallory Park.*
(Bottom) *Hard hitting point-of-sale display.*

Join The Club

- Money-off voucher book for other products.
- FREE stickers, licence holder and wall poster.
- Slick 50 clothing and goodies at special member's prices.

Other special facilities available only to members – see inside for full details.

You'll be miles better off with Slick 50 – the modern way to

- ★ Increased mechanical efficiency
- ★ Improved fuel consumption
- ★ Better performance
- ★ Reduced Friction
- ★ Less wear and tear, particularly from cold start up
- ★ Quieter running
- ★ Guard against internal corrosion
- ★ Increased turbo charger reliability
- ★ Reduced harmful exhaust emissions.

Did you know?
PTFE was formulated as a dry lubricant for use in space. Now Slick 50 allows you to make use of space-age technology to make your car run smoother, quieter and more economically.
Whatever you drive, you'll be miles better off with Slick 50

Made in England for
Petrolon (UK) Ltd.

PETROLON

Under Licence from Socopar Ltd.

Sole Distributors for the U.K.

MITCHELL
Marketing

Mitchell Marketing Limited
140 Leicester Road
Wigston
Leicester LE8 1DS
Telephone: (0533) 881522
Telex: 341401 (J.J.)
Fax: (0533) 813235

Slick 50 is the
Registered Trademark
of Socopar Ltd.

STARTING YOUR ENGINE IS A TERRIBLE THING TO DO.

SLICK 50

(Above) *Members paid just £5 for life including "technical hotline".*

Chris Mitchell, supremo of Mitchell Marketing and Peter Hale, Senior Buyer of Halfords achieved a lifetime ambition and a "world record" on the run from John O'Groats to Lands End. AAR is proud to have been a sponsor.

Going downhill -Fast!

A slick performance! From John O'Groats to Lands End in five minutes less than the previous record held by a Ferrari 308 GTB. Eight hundred and eighty miles in about the same times as it takes for the hour hand to go once around the clock.

Why? Well, Chris Mitchell and Peter Hale can give you no better reason than that they have always wanted to drive "downhill" from the North of Scotland to the very Western tip of England quicker than anyone has driven it before.

The chosen vehicle was a well prepared Toyota MR2. It acquitted itself admirably. Throughout the ordeal it never murmured or showed signs of fading. Indeed when the intrepid pair reached their Cornish goal both Hale and Mitchell were eager to conquer new records.

Eight hundred and eighty miles in the hours of daylight is a considerable achievement. But what was equally noteworthy was the very modest fuel consumption. Overall, the 1600cc engine average 27.8 mpg. And during the Scottish section the pair were putting on a respectably brisk pace.

The 27.8 mpg is considerably better than the 20 mpg a leading motoring magazine accomplished when subjecting its Toyota MR2 to prolonged "hard driving".

So pleased are the Mitchell-Hale team with MR2's performance that they have thrown down the gauntlet to the aftermarket for anyone in a 1600cc car to better both their time and their fuel consumption.

Historically, the run from John O'Groats to Lands End has attracted many record seekers. Paratroopers on the march, cyclists, and even pram pushers have all tried to shave minutes off the previous best.

What is mysterious is why

The men (above) and the machine (below), Chris Mitchell and Peter Hale with their Toyota MR2.

it should be John O'Groats that draws towards it the fastest and most competitive of any field. The humble village is not even the most northerly point in the mainland British Isles, but somehow the name has acquired a mystique and magic of its own.

But at 5.30am on the morning of Sunday 27th October Mitchell and Hale found the hallowed spot a little less than romantic. Everything was closed and the farmer's wife with whom they had arranged breakfast for the morn of the historic attempt was fast asleep in her bed and had forgotten to provide any milk for their cornflakes, tea, and other vi-

tal components to a traditional hearty foundation to the day.

Food was important. In the total run there were only 24 minutes of stoppages, so there was no opportunity to stop for a decent lunch. There was barely a moment to re-fuel and make the body comfortable.

During the drive Mars bars provided the main form of nourishment. The nutritional value of this confectionery might be disputed but there is nothing quite equivalent to a Mars bar for a lift when the fatigue begins to show.

Mercifully the roads were generally clear. It was only when the Mitchell-Hale

team hit the county of Cornwall that the twisting roads and locals began to raise the frustration level.

There were compensations. During the last hour the Slik 50 car was piloted through the villages of Mitchell and Hayle (OK, so the spelling of Hale was not quite up to the mark, but what do you expect in rural areas!).

With the clocks going back

on the Sunday of this historic run the Sun had, of course, plunged beneath the Western horizon by the time the First and Last House was reached.

To celebrate Chris Mitchell and Peter Hale celebrated in time honoured motorsport manner. Champagne corks popped, but it is not recorded if the spray from the Moët et Chandon met that of the Atlantic breakers.

On Monday the record smashing pair decided to make their way back to the Midlands at a canter rather than a gallop.

But you cannot escape the aftermarket. While enjoying lunch at the Ship Inn at Mevigissey two ladies sat at the adjoining bench. Conversation began. "Where have you come from"? "Oh, John O'Groats".

"Are you anything to do with the accessory and parts trade?"

"Yes, why do you ask?"

"Well, we have just retired from running an accessory shop". Talk then be-

came more animated as our heroes modestly outlined their achievement.

AAR congratulates the pair and wishes them every success should they consider further adventures. How about the Mille Miglia? But whatever they choose you can be certain that Slik 50 will be part of the engines preparation as it was on this charge from John O'Groats to Lands End.

Trade press reluctantly approved.

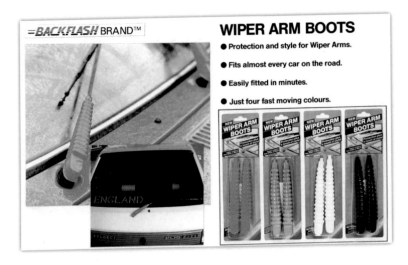

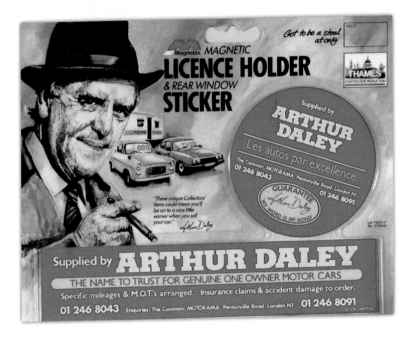

(Bottom) *With a warranty from Arthur Daley what more could you wish for?*

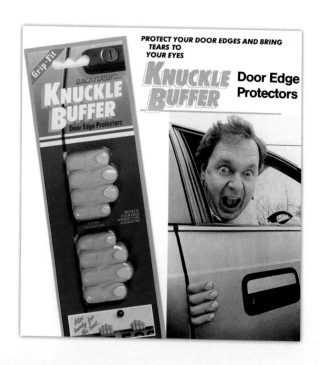

(Top) *Ouch!*
(Bottom) *The Italian look for stick-on "designer dirt".*

Carlo Carlini, a big designer talent.

SLICK OPERATOR

Chris Mitchell, the man behind the success of Slick 50, Backflash and Carlini, has sold out. But, as he tells Murdo Morrison, he has no plans to ditch the industry for good.

"Sold" to America.

months. It was now October 1980 and although I had nothing to sell except my experience in the trade, I set up Mitchell Marketing Ltd, in a back room at home.

My second visit to Vegas for the big show was when jobless, I thought I should try and sell my UK trade experience to the Americans, including buying and selling on an agency basis. Flying out rather more slowly and economically than last time, I found myself next to another exhibitor on the last hop from Los Angeles to Las Vegas, a fellow businessman I had met at trade events before.

He told me that he had no hotel for the first night but was booked into one of the big ones for the rest of the show. I was in exactly the same boat, with Caesar's Palace booked after the first night, but I also had nowhere to sleep initially. We agreed to share a twin room anywhere we could find at short notice, just to crash out briefly. Our taxi driver helpfully dropped us at a rather basic looking downtown hotel. We checked in blearily and quickly fell asleep.

On waking, I discovered that my wallet, briefcase, luggage, samples and clothes had all gone, but my passport had been thankfully left on the dressing table. Help! We'd been robbed! All I had left was my pyjamas. My colleague, further from the door, had not had as much taken and wisely always slept with his wallet under the pillow.

Reception staff were completely uninterested and referred us to the police department, who helpfully pointed out that, having not put on the door safety chain, it was lucky we hadn't woken up during the theft, or we would be dead. My friend did some basic clothes shopping for me and lent me some cash. On leaving the hotel we noticed the reception area was draped with bored-looking women in leotards lounging on couches and finally realised it wasn't just a hotel. I quickly lost motivation when the exhibitions opened and without money, samples, or possessions somehow made my way back to the UK.

SEVEN

SMOOTH OPERATORS

O F ALL THE MANY AND VARIED SUPPLIERS AT RSA, only one had always had unfilled potential – a firm called Finnigan's Paints Ltd, manufacturing Hammerite Paint and Waxoyl Rustproofer up in Prudhoe, Northumberland. Although they had two excellent products, the problem was that they offered no workable level of trade discount, so the shops and wholesalers had virtually no incentive to stock them. Their products were in continual demand, highly effective and well regarded by the public. However, as there was little profit in it for the trade, there was none of their stuff in the shops, so they had never really taken off. They had therefore always supplied retail customers by direct mail order, advertising in *Exchange and Mart* and around 20 titles of monthly motoring magazine.

Hammerite came about because Alan Forster, an industrial chemist, had been a 'radio ham'. All the hams used to keep their equipment on Dexion racking and needed a fancy coating to smarten up the racks, which were otherwise rather ugly and often set up in the family living room. Alan had developed a paint, which on application, dried very quickly to a handsome hammer finish. It turned out that it didn't need an undercoat and also prevented the development of rust on railings, gates and all types of metal.

Their other product, Waxoyl, was an excellent underbody and car cavity rustproofer, with a well-established track record and much used by those in the know. It was initially sold through ham radio magazines by mail order and then spread into the motoring market. Even in 2020, the word Waxoyl is used in classified adverts selling cars as "... fully Waxoyled" – so it has now become a generic!

The firm's income came via postal orders or cheques, with all goods dispatched by parcel post only. A repeat of the 1970 postal strike was imminent, and I knew that Alan and his wife, who were 50:50 shareholders, would be desperately worried about the future of their business. So a trip to Prudhoe and lunch at the single table in their favourite chip shop, Finnigan's Fish 'n' Chips (hence the name of their firm) resulted a month later in a deal. Mitchell Marketing would take on national sales by setting up a team of agents and would try to get the already popular and much demanded products put on the shelf by the major outlets and all shops right across the UK, as well, of course, as the cash and carries. In short, our job was simply to expose their range properly to the danger of being bought!

To do this, at the end of 1980, I negotiated a five-year, exclusive sales agency and marketing deal, subject to year on year increases. They had to make the stuff, dispatch it, extend credit to the trade and fund a big marketing and PR campaign steered by Mitchell Marketing. But we had to actually sell it. The reward of course was a very decent commission on sales, which we shared with my newly created agents' network.

Our first action was to nearly double the retail price to allow a proper trade discount structure, redesign everything and repackage all products under the complete control of Mitchell Marketing. We also arranged to supply the trade on the sort of terms they would expect from other suppliers. So, the big task was to sell the stock to the trade, starting in February 1981. Up to then Finnigan's sales had been well under £1m per annum, with most of the products in plain tins with brown paper wrappers.

The factory was in Prudhoe village, 15 miles west of Newcastle. It mainly boasted the world's largest toilet roll factory, with next door the less famous Waxoyl works. Housed in this old factory were around 12 staff, mainly women, six of whom sat on three-legged milking stools below huge vats of Hammerite paint. Their job was to take an empty tin from the tray to the left, open the tap, fill the tin and place it in the tray to their right, where someone else with a hammer knocked on the lids. Three colours were then being produced: silver, black and mid-blue. Occupying the other half of the factory were the huge Waxoyl mixing tanks.

Very soon the trade found there was a profit to be made at last, both from Hammerite and Waxoyl. The new packaging looked good too, so they bought it – by the lorry load. The public of course, now relieved of the burden of posting off cheques and postal orders and having found it at last on the shelves, lapped it up. Within a few months we had increased sales so much that the factory needed serious modernisation. Amusingly, when I asked the boss to put on a night shift to cope with demand he told me he would ask the 4pm ladies to stay until 7pm!

So we were off and within a year the main trade magazine readers had voted Waxoyl 'Profit Maker of the Year' for 1982. Car manufacturers were the greatest help of course by making cars with little rust protection. Rust formed so quickly under most makes of car that Finnigan's products became the motorist's best friend. By now we were also supplying Aston-Martin-Lagonda for their production line at Newport Pagnell.

The Falklands war proved a good story for my small sales force when RAF Strike Command started buying Waxoyl. It turned out that the undercarriage for the Harrier Jump Jets was very susceptible to salt water spray. A Waxoyl treatment provided the necessary protection to improve combat reliability and to bring the aircraft up to Sea Harrier anti-corrosion specification.

Another wartime story also helped – although only used word of mouth by our sales force – this time going back to the Second World War. The local aircraft reclamation society had recently retrieved a Spitfire from a bog including, sadly, the pilot, who had gone down with his aircraft during the 1940s.

The pilot's rubber oxygen mask and tubing and leather flying helmet were intact, but in a sorry state, as was his transparent map case and map. The society had heard of the preservative powers of locally made Waxoyl and asked if they could put all his equipment into a big bucket of Waxoyl to see what happened in terms of hopefully preserving it. Two weeks later, everything was almost as new and the colours on the paper/linen map were plain to see. As part of the sales pitch in the early days it helped to put our competition in the shade.

As Profit Maker of the Year again the following year (1983) we now had eight commission agents, plus distribution in all shops and good exposure right across 300 Halfords' stores. I was no longer operating from a room at home, as a friend had very kindly lent me an office in his family factory and I had taken on a secretary – a man, unusually. He was one of few people who knew how to work one of the first Apple computers and we had one – big breakthrough. An odd chap though: his hobby was posting out mail order lavender bags via a women's magazine. He also taught Tai-Kwando in the car park at lunchtime to young boys. It was not a tale that ended well …

Before very long Mitchell Marketing had moved out into four rented rooms above a shop called Epic Accessories in Oadby Leicester, (very much in business today) and our letterhead grandly called our little backdoor entrance "Hammerite House". Now we had national distribution and saturation coverage there was nothing to stop us feeding other products from Mitchell Marketing into the pipeline in our own right and the agents were ready to snap anything up.

In one of the trade magazines I read that a young toyshop assistant in Melton Mowbray had designed an item of rear screen styling and had even sold a few to his local accessory shops. It was simply a horizontal series of red stripes sliced up in such a way as to read Mini, or Fiesta, with a red parallel stripe either side. It looked really sexy and didn't impede rear vision, so I arranged to see him and for the sum of £500 bought the rights to his idea, thus allowing him to buy a new scooter.

Mitchell Marketing branded the product 'Backflash' and began mass production, starting with such makes as Ford, GTI and Cortina, in dramatic packaging, for a cost of 70p and a retail price of £5.99. Backflash was an immediate success and the more were visible on rear windows the more we sold. Eventually we had 40 titles in red or white and it was difficult to drive anywhere without spotting one. We actually offered a prize to the agent who saw the most Backflashes on a car in any one day and the winner counted 25 in Belfast. We even did an 007 version, paired with a relaunch of Bulletholes, all properly licensed this time. Unfortunately it coincided with the terrible shootings in Dunblane, which rather ended that version. We also did specials, such as Spurs or Chelsea, for £16, made in 14 days. Luckily, having Finnigan's as our main earner with their two serious brands, we could justify handling much less worthy items.

When we had needed to launch the 'Shot up Spy' 007 edition, including Bulletholes in the Backflash range, we looked for a 007 registration number to buy for my car for photographic purposes. Nothing came up, until one day we spotted SPY 999 for sale in the Sunday Times. We snapped it up and it has since been on about 30 cars. In those days filling up with petrol when using one of the old 'scrub-over' credit card machines, one was always asked for the registration number for the cashier to write on the slip. Many were the times cashiers said, "Great number, is it to do with your job mate?" I always made a pretence of clamming up with a cautionary finger to the lips, or a mention of the Official Secrets Act, leaving the cashier open-mouthed.

Windscreen wipers couldn't be left untouched and we soon took on the exclusive distributorship for a pair of ribbed, soft plastic sleeves to be slid down the wiper arm in three colourways. The trade predictably called them 'wiper arm condoms'. These served no practical purpose, but gave flies a gentler death.

The big money-spinners were still the Hammerite paint range and the brand leading Waxoyl rust preventer, providing a nice big monthly income with very low overheads, as all the manufacturing distribution and invoicing was done from Prudhoe. Invoiced sales were now well over £5m. Things at the factory were always a little unpredictable and I turned up one day to be introduced to a very attractive young woman who informed me that she was the new marketing director. Somewhat taken aback, since that was contractually very much our job, I asked what were her qualifications? She replied that she had a degree in Victorian melodrama and had been the sales rep for *Exchange and Mart* magazine. Since it was Alan and not his 50% shareholding wife who had made the appointment, I could feel some seismic marital happenings on the horizon, so I viewed it as my duty to divert her attentions during subsequent overnight visits. Soon after, she returned to London and eventually things calmed down.

However, abruptly one day, six months after she went, one of the agents phoned up: did we know that Finnigan's was selling out? Wow, although I had been visiting the factory at least once every three weeks for two years, not a word about this was mentioned. They soon admitted that a large cash offer for the whole business had come from the Hunting Group, who were into oil exploration and defence and it was such a good offer that the Forsters were planning to retire. Since there were two years of our contract left to run, a decent payout was agreed, but most of my reliable income had largely disappeared overnight and I had about a year before the money ran out. So, we had an office, a team of commission agents and all the levers of national distribution, but suddenly, no main product.

Every summer *CAT* magazine (*Car and Accessory Trader* – nothing to do with cats) hosted a cricket match at the old Sihillians' ground near Solihull. The two teams were the motor accessory manufacturers v the motor accessory distributors. The main focus, other than cricket, was networking around a boozy lunch and the strawberry tea – all very nice, mingling in our whites, but also vital for Mitchell Marketing in August 1984, as we needed a product.

Chatting with the wicketkeeper, Harry Toms, an unfamiliar face, I gathered he had an American product that was going nowhere, an oil additive that was supposedly big in the States. He'd had the rights for this product for a year but had only sold about 100 tins in the UK and was about to give up. It was called Slick-50, (yuck, what a name, I thought) and it was three times the cost of STP, the absolute all-out market leader. I was walking away when he added, "By the way it's a permanent treatment, not one you have to put in every oil change and it uses Teflon. I was intrigued.

Harry persuaded me to have lunch with him the following week to discuss Slick-50 and I heard about the growth in manufacture of PTFE (polytetrafluoroethylene), marketed by ICI as Teflon for non-stick frying pans. Evidently the need for a solid lubricant came from the space race. Having a wet lubricant like oil on moving parts such as hinges, in a weightless atmosphere meant it just drifted off the surfaces. But PTFE baked onto surfaces during manufacture left a permanent lubricant.

At that stage in the lunch I was getting well lubricated as well, especially when Harry said that PTFE was "the slipperiest substance known to man". Once added to the hot engine of a car and then left to run for 30 minutes it left this amazing permanent coating on all the moving parts for the life of the engine. All existing oil additives like STP had to be added at every single oil change. Slick-50 was permanent, there for the life of the engine and referred to quite differently as an 'engine treatment', NOT just an oil additive.

By now I was getting quite excited, especially as the unique selling points were more power and better economy, resulting from the big reduction of friction. The packaging was dreadful, public awareness was nil, I didn't like the 'spivvy' product name and being three times costlier than the competition wasn't helpful, but Harry still persuaded me to go to London with him to see his rich backer (who was about to back out) simply to have a conversation about any ideas I might have.

Sten Ahlberg and his wife Britta were a delightful Swedish couple. He was a retired, mega-wealthy industrialist and she had been a Swedish cabinet minister. They owned an amazing penthouse apartment, sandwiched between two well-guarded foreign embassies and overlooking Kensington Gardens, with Picasso works on the walls. I outlined what needed to be done to relaunch the product and insisted that to succeed they needed to think about putting £50,000 behind it, to be spent by Mitchell Marketing and that I would need an agreement in perpetuity to handle the product, subject to year on year sales always increasing.

Slick-50 was basically an American import from Petrolon Inc., based in Houston Texas, selling over there only through garage forecourts in one pint, rip top cans. It was a fairly stagnant brand and the name couldn't be changed, but otherwise we had complete freedom to recreate the brand for the British market and a decent budget behind us to finance it, plus the carrot of Holland, Belgium and Switzerland to take on if the launch was successful. Our role was to recreate the brand, carry the stock, pack, dispatch and invoice it and of course, sell it. So we did the deal – after all, I had the time and the connections – and it was all systems GO.

The key was to persuade Halfords to stock Slick-50 in every single branch, as long as they had a sole mention in all the national press adverts and so the first quarter page ads appeared in *The Daily Mail* in March 1985. Then, since the trade as a whole didn't like the idea of Halfords having it all to themselves, all the independents and most of the big cash and carry chains decided to stock it too. After all, I had helped them make a lot of money with Waxoyl and Hammerite. So there we were, quite quickly, with national distribution.

We now had to move to a proper warehouse in Wigston, Leicester, and seeing a huge articulated lorry stacked two high with pallets of Slick-50 leaving the yard for Halfords' first stock order was a memorable sight. Overall demand levels justified increasing the ad spend and by 1986 we were on television during the World Cup football ad breaks, as well as during *Coronation Street,* with a 30-second commercial, fronted by rally driver Roger Clark, Britain's greatest rally driver at the time.

The newly leased premises proved perfect for our purpose, comprising a spacious, first floor set of offices and a handsomely oak-panelled boardroom, plus a decent-sized warehouse at the rear. By then I had decided on the company motto, 'Patience is not a virtue', which I like to think stood us in good stead. Running a tight ship with minimum overheads was always a crucial part of the company doctrine, although we never stinted on advertising or promotional expenditure. However, there were certain fairly firm rules we adopted, such as no outgoing phone calls before 1pm, only essential ones during the afternoon and calls to the sales force at their homes always after 6pm. (Remember, no mobiles then.) The telephone charging system at that time was such that afternoon calls were half the price of those in the morning, with evening calls cheaper still.

We had a very smart stair carpet leading up the circular staircase to our offices and after a year or so it was getting very worn down the middle due to heavy use. What seemed to cause some amusement was the notice at the bottom directing people to use the left hand side going up and the opposite side going down, thereby evening out the wear, but to be fair, in those days a new carpet would have cost the equivalent of a quarter page ad in *The Sun*! The office staff thought I was going a bit far with the directive of cutting Post-It notes in half, so that one didn't last long ... But on the plus side, our reps were the first to be equipped with new BMWs rather than the traditional reps' Fords and our very best sales agent earned more than I paid myself one year with his substantial and very well deserved commission.

I made many visits to Halfords' head office at Redditch to see their senior buyer, Peter Hale. We often started with a lavish lunch at a nearby Italian restaurant, which was his special favourite. Plenty of wine was consumed, with port and cheese afterwards, before we went back to his office, whereupon he happily signed the next month's buying orders. By now Halfords was also stocking the whole Backflash range, as well as all our other lines and we were their sole supplier for L plates and tax disc holders. But Slick-50 was the big one.

One memorable year they hosted a major conference for key suppliers up in Aviemore, where we were all put up for the night, having been flown up in specially chartered aircraft to enjoy a Burns night and haggis feast followed by a sales presentation. Next day we boarded the plane to return. As we climbed the steps to the aircraft we were each handed a large envelope and on sitting down and reading the contents, I saw it was basically a request for a substantial advertising contribution for the following year. I was aware that there is no such thing as a free lunch, but was horrified to see that Mitchell marketing was being asked for £200,000 as our contribution. Ashen faced, I turned to the companion sitting on my left, the top man from Castrol Oil. He was beaming, as he said their contribution had dropped right down to £20,000. To my huge relief it transpired that our envelopes had somehow got swapped over!

It turned out during our Halfords lunches that one of buyer Peter's great ambitions was to break the record for driving from John O'Groats to Lands End in a car and we both saw this as an example of demonstrating the mpg economy benefits of Slick-50. So, driving my Toyota MR2, we went for it, starting at the north end in October 1985. Our time was 11 hours 48 minutes for the total 880 miles (before the M5 was complete) and we broke the speed limit in 20 counties, finishing sitting on the rocks at Lands End drinking champagne. Our average speed was 74mph including, as the MR2 had a rather small tank, five brief fuel stops! Our sustenance was Mars Bars and Perrier water, with loo visits as the fuel was going in. My brother, a solicitor, made sure that we didn't publicise this high-speed journey until a fortnight later, to avoid prosecution.

This certainly helped with the product's reputation because the mpg was 42 miles to the gallon, which was the real excuse for doing it – and the escapade certainly helped with the product's reputation. Driving back home, my co-driver confessed he was bored with his job of senior buyer at Halfords and was ready for a change. So within a few months he was sales director for Mitchell Marketing and he was a huge asset – a perfect example of poacher turned gamekeeper. It was the talk of the trade.

EIGHT

END OF AN ERA

R ALLY DRIVER ROGER CLARK, BY NOW INTERNATIONALLY famous, had become the 'product ambassador' for Slick-50 and agreed to do a publicity stunt at Leicestershire's local Mallory Park racing circuit, only two miles from his house and three miles from his favourite pub, the Bulls Head, near Peckleton. The idea was to dramatically demonstrate how a Slick-50 treated engine would still keep going, even if the oil was lost. For the rally boys, on a rock-strewn special stage, getting a cracked sump could wreck their chances with an engine blow up, so proving the protective abilities of Slick 50 would be good publicity.

We had two cars on the start line at Mallory Park at 2pm that afternoon. One was my secretary's rather high mileage Renault without any Slick-50 treatment and the other was a Fiat Strada, which had been thoroughly treated with Slick-50 and been used by one of the reps. We had an RAC observer there to see fair play and to watch both sumps being emptied on the start line with the removed sump plugs kept in the RAC observer's pocket. So, two cars on the start line with no engine oil in either and the flag was dropped. Roger drove the Slick-50 treated car and a motoring journalist drove the untreated car. We had promised St John Ambulance (who were always generously in attendance at motor sport events) the sum of £10 for every lap completed by Roger with no engine oil.

The two cars set off to maintain a carefully monitored and agreed 50mph. After one lap my secretary's car's engine went bang in a cloud of black smoke. (A new engine had already been promised.) Roger was starting to yawn after ten boring laps, then 20 laps, then 30 laps, when, passing the pits, he shouted, "When can I stop?" My reply was, "Keep going".

At 40 laps he was becoming visibly agitated. I happened to know he had spent lunchtime sinking pints at his usual pub, so on his next lap I called, "Make it 50 laps and finish". He duly stopped and rushed off to the loo – and so we lifted the bonnet. The engine was extremely hot and the metal was ticking like a grandfather clock after 50 oil-free miles, but we eventually refilled it and one of the reps then used it for a further six months. Our PR company squeezed masses of publicity from the stunt, which was remembered for many years afterwards. My secretary got her new engine and St John's Ambulance received their cheque for £500.

By now our relationship with Halfords was very strong and their buying department was using us as a filter to save themselves wasting time with 'mad inventors' with all sorts of crackpot product ideas. They used to initially pass them on to us at the rate of one or two a month and our small 'Dragon's Den' committee would get the optimistic entrepreneur to visit us, usually resulting in a thumbs down. But occasionally there was a good one, so being able to offer national distribution we did an immediate deal and eventually re-presented the revamped products to Halfords and the rest of the trade as part of our product line-up.

Products from China were now starting to make inroads and one enterprising gentleman came in front of our new product committee with 'The Bubble Potty'. He had rashly invested in 20,000 of these and was keen to have us take it on for national distribution.

It was basically a half size pink upside-down inflatable top hat without the rim, and came in a little pink wallet beautifully blister packed, with some disposable liners, and an illustration of a child in a car precariously perched on it.

Translations in those days left a lot to be desired, but I well remember some of the wording on the packaging, such as, "For lady to blow up quickly" and "When liner bag filled, tie knot and throw out window" and finally, "Adult can use as shower hat". Surprisingly, our committee gave it the thumbs down!

Thames Television's *Minder* series was near the top of the viewing figures, with the dubious secondhand car salesman 'Arfur' Daley played by George Cole, assisted by Dennis Waterman as his shifty sidekick. We approached Thames with a deal to sell a tax-disc holder and a rear window sticker, skin-wrapped together and branded as Arthur Daley Motors. They agreed a licence deal and we went into production. Both items proudly bore the far-from-truthful Arthur Daley Motors legend 'My Word is My Bond' and a phone number, which, anyone who dialled the number found was 'Dial a Recipe'. The product sold steadily for years and I was even invited to watch the filming of the very last episode and to meet the stars, George Cole and Dennis Waterman, on set. Those who used to watch it will be as surprised as I was to find that the sleazy basement Winchester Club was actually filmed halfway up an office block in Hammersmith.

THE SLICK-50 CHAMPIONSHIP

We now had full distribution for Slick-50 and needing to boost sales, we got talked into sponsoring a Toyota racing saloon car driven by Andy Ackerley. We paid £10,000 for his season's racing and although the car was covered with Slick-50 decals, no victories ensued. We then sponsored the very up-and-coming Formula One driver Roland Ratzenburger in a saloon car race driving a BMW M3, mainly sponsored by motor sporting accessory dealers,

'Demon Tweeks', which for a one-off race cost £5000, but he sadly didn't win. Even more sadly, he was killed soon after at the very same F1 Italian Grand Prix weekend at Imola where Ayrton Senna lost his life – a disastrous period for racing drivers.

We were then approached by the BRSCC (British Racing and Sports Car Club) and offered a complete championship with our name on it for a two-year period. For £10,000 per annum it would be called 'The Slick-50 Road-going Saloon Car Championship' and have a grid of up to 25 cars under 3-litres and another grid for the big bangers over 3-litres; again 25 cars. They would all carry big Slick-50 logos and in addition we could use our own commentator to slip in all the right product remarks, have a page in the programme and use our own special liveried car (actually my Jaguar with magnetic signs on the doors) to open and close the track between each race. It was a no-brainer for £10,000 per annum, with 50 cars at ten meetings a year. The championship eventually ran for eight years on circuits across the country, plus an annual overseas race at Zandvoort in Holland and helped to build up a huge following for the product. And let's not forget Lewis Hamilton and Jenson Button, whose earliest trophy wins were in the Slick-50 Ford British Kart Championships!

In 1989 we decided to give things a real boost with a national television campaign. To do it properly cost £250,000 and the bank drew the line at funding something without any material asset base as collateral. All we had was a large photocopier and some stock, so reluctantly I had to put our family house up as security. Quite a decision to make, as I had remarried some years before and now also had two sturdy teenage stepsons depending on me. But as sales of Slick-50 always went up in direct proportion to the ad-spend, I was confident, as was our ad agency – "Grey", headed by Mike Slessor.

The key part at the end of the TV ad involved our brand ambassador Roger Clark at Mallory Park circuit. Dressed in his racing overalls, he was filmed walking confidently towards the camera, brandishing a pack of Slick-50. He then stopped and announced, "I've always used Slick-50 in my cars. You should too."

Roger was the nicest and most modest of men, as well as being the UK's top rally driver for many years, but he had a very quiet personality, so didn't find this at all easy. We repeated endless takes and finished the day without total confidence in the result. In fact his voice on the replays sounded so unconvincing that the agency ultimately resorted to recording a voice-over artist in a professional overdub, copying Roger's voice characteristics for the actual advert.

We had booked a prominent corner stand at the next Earls Court trade show to launch the campaign and the advert was running on a loop on a TV monitor at the very front of the stand. Roger attended the first day and immediately stopped to watch the video as he walked onto the stand. "Wow, I'm so relieved it's come out okay", he said. "I thought I had cocked it up." We never told him. The campaign was a huge success, sales went further through the roof – and thankfully the bank let me have back the deeds to my own roof, with the house beneath it.

The 1980s were a great time for car bodywork styling, mainly self-adhesive and running the length of the car. The biggest producer was Stylistic, with a huge range of full-length pinstripes in many widths and colours, as well as a range of very artistic, graphic stick-on styling to quite radically jazz up and restyle the often rather slab-sided bodywork of the day.

In fact Stylistic dominated this lucrative market with big profit margins for all until Mitchell Marketing decided to enter the market. Italians had always been seen as leaders in style and design, so what better name than 'Carlo Carlini' to launch a new range of car bodywork styling graphics? The packaging carried images of the Colosseum and St Peters in Rome, Pisa's Leaning Tower and the Venice skyline. The colour scheme for the logo was mainly green, white and red, the Italian national colours. Our PR company put out vague press releases about the mystery man Carlo Carlini himself, who "may be visiting the next accessory show." The trade, including Halfords, took the substantial new range in quite happily. As it happened, I was in fact Mr. Carlini; the products were designed in Leicester and made in Walsall.

For many years the car manufacturers and all the associated branches of the motor and component trade annually used The Earls Court Exhibition Centre. Although demolished in 2010, it was a massive three-story concrete structure, famous for hosting not only the International Motor Show but also the Boat Show. It boasted a huge lake in the middle of the ground floor, which could float a small fleet of the latest yachts and was of course boarded over for most exhibitions. The big international shows in those days were usually for two weeks and a real endurance course.

The Motor Show occupied all three floors, with cars taking up the ground floor, the major components and parts brands the first floor balcony area, with motor accessories the very wide balconied top floor. Heat rises, so the centre void acted as an invisible vortex of heat and dust, which mainly seemed to land on the top floor exhibitors. Most of the public and the motor traders in the UK loved to visit for the excuse of a night out in town with a bit of business thrown in, so it was always very crowded around the cars downstairs, but the top floor exhibitors needed to lure the trade buyers onto their stands to see the latest gadgets and place nice big orders.

Booze and women usually did the trick and many stands displayed glamorous girls, scantily dressed – after all it was very hot up there – to welcome the traders and guide them into the built in bar 'lounge' at the back, to then be plied with gin and tonic. First free drinks were usually served at 10am when the stands opened and when the show closed we all fell exhausted into the nearest bars and restaurants, except for the legendary few hell-raising exhibitors who always went clubbing.

Crowning glory moments at Earls Court included 1984 when we were on the top floor, as usual with all the other accessory and component people. Ready for a change of scenery after a busy morning on the stand, I headed down to the ground floor to hanker over a few motorcars. Passing the Lotus stand I couldn't resist a close-up of the new convertible Lotus Elan. In those days the stands weren't all fenced off against the inquisitive hordes as they are today and opening the door, I slipped into the cockpit to get a feel of the driving position. Just then, a chap in a smart dark suit approached and thinking he was a salesman I asked him about the engine output. He seemed somewhat nonplussed and in fact didn't have a clue, but as he somewhat firmly asked me to kindly climb out, I spotted a swathe of arc lights being hurriedly set up around the perimeter of the stand. Next, who should walk purposefully towards that very car but Princess Diana? To this day I shall treasure the smile she beamed my way as she slid her shapely legs under the steering wheel I had just been grasping and shimmied into the seat I had warmed for her. I was soon back at work upstairs – needless to say, somewhat dazzled by my Royal encounter.

For the earlier two thirds of my career I went to Earls Court as a buyer, spending two days cruising the stands to spot any new products, particularly from Far Eastern exhibitors who were starting to make an impact. In later years I went as an exhibitor and made many new friends in the trade. Practical jokes abounded and the year that we launched the Waxoyl pressurised 2-litre, refillable spray-can was fun. The can had a hand pump on the top to force the sticky fluid down a tube into a car's cavities. Of course, for the show we had empty display cans, but when filled with water and pumped up they had a considerable range. As the stands had no ceilings, it was therefore easy to aim a refreshing spray on to certain exhibitors, maybe ten stands away. Many of them complained to the show organisers, reporting that the roof was leaking.

A few years into the Slick-50 expansion, the overall licence holder for the brand in Europe, John Green, asked me over to The French Riviera for a Mediterranean cruise, leaving from Monaco on his yacht. John lived with his wife and daughters in a beautiful apartment in Monte Carlo (as it happened sharing an adjacent balcony with Ringo Starr, who waved at me one day).

John asked me to meet him at Nice Heliport, whence we helicoptered to Monaco with his family and boarded his brand new, 40-foot, aluminium-hulled, Swan yacht, which I reckoned had been funded by his Slick-50 sales to Mitchell Marketing! He had hired a professional skipper for the three-day maiden voyage, to show him the ropes and it was a scorching day as we cleared the harbour aiming for Sardinia. John then said, "Who'd like a drink?" The skipper and I together replied, "A beer please", only to be told that the family had always been teetotal and there was only orange squash or coke on board. I bet our faces were a picture.

In 1991 one of our suppliers was visiting our office on his annual visit from Exeter. Our 'works canteen', The Star and Garter pub in Wigston, three doors up the road, was the regular place for a business lunch and we sat there trying to think up new product ideas. I had earlier seen a car that some joker had equipped with an obviously dummy arm hanging out of the boot. So why not make up some clip-on knuckles to go on the trailing edge of the boot lid? This perfect 'body in the boot trying to escape' effect we came up with had a highly practical function and really sold as a pair of very effective door buffers to protect the door edges in a brick garage or car park. They sold like crazy and were my final product – so from Bulletholes to Knuckle Buffers – but thankfully with much useful and worthwhile stuff in the intervening years.

Eventually, in November 1991, Petrolon Inc., in Houston, Texas, as the ultimate Slick 50 licensees and brand owners, had suddenly realized that the UK was outselling the US. They decided they wanted to take a proper look at our operation and to meet the people involved in the marketing. Their top team of four, led by cigar-smoking president William Jeter III, duly arrived at Gatwick Airport. They asked for the best hotel near the airport, so we booked them into Gravetye Manor, a superb five-star hotel in glorious grounds.

After check-in they wanted "one of your proper English teas" and settled in the oak-panelled drawing room for us all to be served by waitresses in full Victorian-style dress with a proper silver service English afternoon tea. The president, finishing his cigar, spotted the handsome silver tea strainer in its dish and commented, "Gee, you English think of everything", then promptly stubbed out his cigar in it.

From Gravetye Manor, the team moved up north the next day to our Wigston HQ and on our best behaviour, we gave them the full sales pitch. In our small way we had proved the power of the brand by entirely different methods to the US and they ultimately wanted world domination without little old Mitchell Marketing controlling a bunch of European countries. Eventually they made me a decent offer, which included everything: Backflash, Carlo Carlini, Arthur Daley – the lot, as I had said it was all or nothing – and six months later, rewinding to the hotel in the opening chapter, the deal was done.

I wasn't really sorry to sell, except that I loved working with my small team. But anyway, as the 1990s had begun, the bulk of the bolt-on accessory business had begun to dwindle dramatically. With more and more new cars coming onto the road, buyers were encouraged to specify the extras to be fitted on the production line, since the car makers wanted the business that the accessory shops had been enjoying. Most of the extras of those 'golden years' were now becoming a standard fit and the DIY skills of the next car buying generation were vanishing.

With European regulations coming in, many products now had to be TuV tested before sale as a safety approved extra. The final nail in the coffin was the insistence by the insurance companies that all additions or modifications to the standard spec should be declared, thus increasing premiums. But, over the 30-year heyday, a lot of people had made a stack of money and enjoyed a barrel of fun, as well as providing some ingenious products and a useful service. Still, nothing lasts forever.

Certainly some mistakes were made over the years and not everything sold like crazy. Much of what was sold during the 'golden' 30 or so years was worthwhile and necessary, but some of it I have to admit was rather frivolous. Strangely, the most important things in my view for cars were fire extinguishers and first-aid kits, yet these were probably the least successful of all the products.

I would say to any youngsters starting out today with not a lot in the way of qualifications, that the most important thing is to be really interested in what you want to do and then throw everything you have at it. Sad to say, but 'family first' won't necessarily help. Total focus will do it and make sure you enjoy the climb, but remember, "patience is not a virtue".

After dabbling in a few other small commercial projects, I have now retired completely and live comfortably in the Leicestershire countryside, although it is rather a shame to order a new car and find that everything is already fitted. But you can, of course, still buy Hammerite, Waxoyl – and Smelly Trees!

ACKNOWLEDGEMENTS

With grateful thanks to Steve Rendle and Melanie Edgell for their very much appreciated help and advice.

AUTOMOTIVE AFTERMARKET SUPPLY-SIDE FIRMS ACTIVE BETWEEN 1960 AND 1990

Autobooks
Airfresh
Aerofan
Arden
Autoplas
Alexander Engineering
Arman
Astrali Wheels

Bluemels
Badger Design
Brown and Geeson
Britover Cibié
Bradex
Britax
Barri
Bell Plastics
Bars Leaks
Bob Soper
Brown Bros
Crypton

ClippaSafe
Club
Carello
Cosmic
Comp Filters
Colortune
Cannon
Corbeau
Carflow
Carplan
Command
Customagic

Duckhams Oils
Davenset
Draper Tools
Davids Isopon
Desmo

Exhaust Ejector
Eversure

Explosafe

Formula Wheels
Freeflow
Fibrepair
Finnigans Paints
Freeline
Fiamm
Fosmin Chemicals
Finilec
Firemaster
Findlay Irvine

Galemaster
Gran Pree
Granville Chemicals

Humbrol
Hartwell
Harry Moss
Haynes Publishing

Hermetite
Hella

Invicta Plastics
Intermotor

John Woolfe Racing
J P Isaacs
Jeenay
John Tailorite

Kenlowe Fans
KL
Kumficar
Karobes
Kangol
Kamasa Tools
Klaxon
Koni

Les Leston
Letco
Link Hampson

Mangoletsi
Metallifacture
Mada
Mary Lamb
Mitchell Marketing
Metro
Motolita
Mountney
Minifin
Mocal
Motopart

Mobelec

Paddy Hopkirk
Petrolon
Plastifilm
Polco
Peco
Plastic Padding

Quickfit70

Renovo
Rainex
Richard Grant
  Accessories
Roland Kerr
Radbourne
Restall
Renamel
Raydyot

Sparto
Sperex
Shraeder
Speedograph
Spectra
Sedan
Solar
Securon
Stadium
Sabre
Selmar
SPQR
Speedwell
Summit

Stylistic
Simoniz
Springall
Spax
Silverline
Solvol Autosol
Sherwood Parsons
STP
Smiths Industries
Sparkrite

Tex
Trend
Tonken
Terry Hunter
Telulog
Tudor
Trimstyle
Trico

Unipart
Universal Products

V C Saunders
Valay

Witter Tow Bars
Wipac
Wolfrace
Wynns
Walpres

Yazaki

 Matador